THE TOWER
SLO-COOK BOOK

THE TOWER
SLO-COOK BOOK

by Annette Yates

W. Foulsham & Co. Ltd.

London · New York · Toronto · Cape Town · Sydney

W. FOULSHAM & COMPANY LIMITED
Yeovil Road, SLOUGH, Berkshire SL1 4JH

ISBN 0-572-00977-1
© W. Foulsham & Co Ltd. 1978

Acknowledgements

Photographer: Regi Conn
Home Economists: Sheila Brotherton
                   Annette Thomas
Designer: Peter Constable
Art Work: Martin Williams

Grateful thanks are extended to Peter Knight (Beaconsfield)
Ltd, 45 London End, Beaconsfield, Bucks., who were kind
enough to supply the following items:
P.28 Copper Grain Measuring Mug
P.34 Wine Glass and Ovenware
P.42 Wine Carafe and Tablecloth
P.43 Tablecloth
P.52 Napkins and Wine Glass
P.60 Wine Carafe
P.66 Copper Measuring Jug and Expanding Mug Rack
P.67 Spice Rack
P.70 Chinese-patterned Ware and Rattan Rice Measure
P.81 Chopping Board and Decorated Coffee Tin
P.85 Wine Glass

CONTENTS

Rating

Throughout the book the recipes have been given a rating.

 means the recipe is easy to prepare

 means the recipe needs a little special care during part or all of the preparation

 means the recipe is suitable for freezing

 means the heat settings and cooking times given in these recipes must *not* be altered

 means recipes should *not* be prepared by the one-step method.

INTRODUCING SLOW COOKING

Slow cooking is a time tested method of successful food preparation. The advent of electrical appliances specifically designed to cope with slow cooking simply adds an up-dated convenience to our busy lifestyles.

Slow cookers have been appreciated in America for some time. Now we too can enjoy the characteristic simmered flavours of both traditional and exotic dishes without the necessity for constant attention. No checking, testing, stirring or turning. Just prepare the ingredients and place them in your Slo-Cooker before leaving home and return to a delicious hot meal. And meals are ready when you are; because of the time range there is little chance of them spoiling even if you are an hour or two late.

Your Slo-Cooker may be used day or night. Cook tomorrow's lunch or breakfast overnight, for example. Use the Slo-Cooker while you are at home, too, and appreciate the feeling of freedom knowing that the meal is cooking itself and the satisfaction that you are also economising on fuel.

The gently simmered (and often inexpensive) dishes that our grandparents prepared can be reproduced with great authenticity in your Slo-Cooker.

I hope you will enjoy the recipes in the pages to follow. Use them as a basis to experiment and develop your own favourite ideas to perfection. You will probably find, like I have, that the Slo-Cooker is best stored on the kitchen work surface where it is always handy for use. It looks very attractive, too. Use your other kitchen equipment to complement it and vice versa. You will find, for example, that some of the recipes will require the use of a blender for liquidising and pans for frying.

Finally, the majority of the recipes in this book are designed for all day cooking; but try those with shorter cooking times, or use the Slo-Cooker on High when you need a meal in a short time or for mid-day, when you have to go out for part of the day, when you want to get on with other chores around the house, or simply when you want a few hours to yourself.

Annette Yates

ABOUT THE RECIPES

The recipes in this book have been thoroughly tested in the Tower Slo-Cooker 3½ litre (6 pint) size. They can however be prepared successfully in any of the slow cookers described in the following pages. Some recipes have been developed to feed 6 or more persons but it is a simple matter to decrease or increase quantities to suit your requirements and the capacity of your slow cooker and cooking times will vary only slightly.

The cooking times given in the recipes have been tested to produce best results. Where a recipe, for example, recommends cooking for 6–8 hours, the recipe will be cooked sufficiently after 6 hours but will still be at its best after 8 hours. Even after that it may be left on the Low setting for a few hours longer without spoiling except if it is indicated at the beginning of the recipe that this is not possible. See symbol on page 5.

The methods of preparation in the recipes have been developed to produce the best results in terms of appearance, texture and flavour. This often includes browning of meat, light sautéeing of vegetables and thickening of liquids before slow cooking. If preparation has to be done early in the morning, before leaving for work, for example, you may prefer to omit any pre-heating of the food before slow cooking. Or, you can prepare the ingredients the evening before, refrigerate them, and place them in the Slo-Cooker next morning, without pre-frying. This is the One-Step method and cooking times will need to be extended, see the separate check-point list.

About your Slo-Cooker

There are several attractive designs of
Slo-Cookers to choose from today. They are all low
wattage appliances designed to cook food gently over
long periods. The wattage used by your Slo-Cooker
will depend on the model; they usually range
between 75–120 watts on Low setting and 120–180
watts on High setting, depending on the
construction. They all, however, consume about as
much electricity as a light bulb which does prove
most economical over a long period.

There are usually two settings available on a
Slo-Cooker; Low and High. Some designs have
On–Off switches and/or indicator lights to show that
the appliance is switched on. The last point is
particularly advantageous when other members of the
household are likely to switch off the Slo-Cooker
without the cook's knowledge.

Slo-Cookers can be divided into two main types:

Type 1 consists of a glazed earthenware pot
permanently fixed into an outer casing of aluminium
or heat-resistant plastic. It is heated by elements
situated round the outside of the pot, between the
pot and the outer casing. This type has a detachable
cord to enable the Slo-Cooker to be taken to the
table.

Type 2 consists of the same basic design as Type
1 but with an earthenware pot which can be removed
from the outer casing. These have the added
advantage that there is less bulk to take to the table
and the pot may be put into the oven or under the
grill to produce crispy toppings. The heating
elements are situated within the outer casing in a
position to heat the base and/or sides of the
earthenware pot.

Choosing a Slo-Cooker

When choosing a Slo-Cooker the following
points may prove helpful.

(a) Choose one with sufficient capacity for your
particular needs. How many do you cook for? Do
you entertain often? Do you cook for the freezer?
Sizes vary from 1.8 litres ($3\frac{1}{4}$ pt) to 3.5 litres (6 pt).

(b) It is a good idea to check that the appliance
has been approved for safety by the British
Electrotechnical Approvals Board (BEAB). If so, this

will be marked on the base of the Slo-Cooker.

(c) Make sure that the manufacturer offers a guarantee.

If a fault should occur or spare parts are required the manufacturer should be contacted. The address will be found in the instruction book for your particular model. In addition, should you have any queries regarding slow cooking, the manufacturer will be pleased to help.

How to care for your Slo-Cooker

Manufacturers' instructions should be followed when washing and cleaning your Slo-Cooker. Before first use, wash the inside of the earthenware pot with warm soapy water, rinse well and dry. Before cleaning always switch off and disconnect the Slo-Cooker from the mains. Empty out the contents, fill the warm Slo-Cooker with hot soapy water and clean with a soft sponge, brush or cloth. Rinse well and wipe dry. Never immerse the cord or plugs in water.

Stubborn food residue is easily removed if the warm Slo-Cooker is left to stand full of hot soapy water for a few minutes. Do not use abrasive pads inside or outside the Slo-Cooker. Clean the outer casing, if necessary, with a soft damp cloth. If the earthenware pot is removable, this may be washed, rinsed and dried in the normal way. The outer casing should not be immersed in water. Never fill the outer casing with water or use it for cooking without the earthenware pot.

Where hard water is used in cooking a 'bloom' (whitish deposit) may appear on the inside of the earthenware pot. This is easily removed with a mild liquid abrasive cleaner. Wipe the earthenware with a little vegetable oil to restore its sparkling

appearance. Take care to avoid chipping the earthenware pot or lid, either with utensils during cooking or against taps etc., during cleaning.

Sudden temperature changes in the earthenware pot should be avoided since the shock could cause it to crack. It is worth remembering these points:

1. Do not put very cold or frozen foods into a heated Slo-Cooker.

2. Removable earthenware pots should not be placed over a naked flame, or if hot, placed on a cold surface.

3. Neither the earthenware pot, nor complete Slo-Cooker should be used to store food in the refrigerator or freezer.

Your Slo-Cooker and your freezer

Your Slo-Cooker and your freezer can be the best of friends. It is a simple matter to prepare large quantities of food in the Slo-Cooker—some to eat immediately and some to freeze for a later date. See the notes about quantities on page 13.

More information about slow cooking and freezing is to be found in the introduction to each section and specific instructions for freezing individual recipes are given at the end of the method where appropriate. Frozen raw meat, poultry and fish must always be thawed thoroughly before slow cooking.

Remember to make use of foods when they are in season; fruits are a good example. Just pop them in the Slo-Cooker with a little water or weak sugar syrup. Cook them then freeze them. Fruit can also be prepared and frozen ready for making jam, jelly or marmalade at a later date.

PREPARING YOUR FOOD

Vegetables take longer to cook than meat. They should therefore, be cut up into thin slices or diced ($\frac{1}{4}$ inch/$\frac{1}{2}$ cm.), placed near the bottom of the Slo-Cooker and immersed in the cooking liquid. If you are browning meat for the same recipe sauté the vegetables for a few minutes too.

Season sparingly; check again just before serving.

Partially thaw frozen vegetables and add them during the final $\frac{1}{2}$-1 hour of the cooking period.

Add milk and cream to savoury dishes during the final half hour since long cooking could cause them to separate.

If your Slo-Cooker is fitted with a removable pot, cooked dishes can be browned under the grill or covered with a topping and crisped in a pre-heated oven.

Add dumplings to soups or stews for the final $\frac{1}{2}$ hour and switch to the High setting for this time.

Use quick-cooking varieties of pasta or rice. Macaroni and lasagne should be softened in boiling water for a few minutes. When using raw rice extra liquid is needed ($\frac{1}{4}$ pt./150 ml./$\frac{2}{3}$ cup liquid for 4 oz./100 g./$\frac{3}{4}$ cup rice). No additional liquid required when cooked rice is used.

Add thickening agents at the start of slow cooking. Alternatively, mix the flour or cornflour with a little cold water and stir it into the ingredients for the final 1–1$\frac{1}{2}$ hours of cooking.

Dry cooking—such as Baked Potatoes—is not advisable since it could damage your Slo-Cooker.

When adapting recipes for slow cooking use about half the normal quantity of liquid since there is less evaporation. Make sure that root vegetables are covered.

Advantages of Slow Cooking

Your Slo-Cooker is superb for preparing soups, stocks, casseroles and stews. Flavours mix, blend and develop to produce concentrated, rich and tasty results. All the flavour is sealed in the pot. Economies are made in terms of fuel, money, effort and time. Fuel savings alone can be as much as 80% on normal cooking times. The efficient built-in insulation means only the food inside the Slo-Cooker heats up, not the whole kitchen.

Foods cooked in the Slo-Cooker remain attractively whole. This is a distinct advantage when cooking fruit, fish, etc. There is no need to turn or stir the food as it is not likely to overcook or boil over or stick and there are no hot spots to cause burning. The gentle heat results in less evaporation of liquids so there is little chance of food drying out. The steam condenses on the lid and returns to the pot. In doing so it forms a seal which retains heat and flavour. The gentle heat also tenderizes tough meat beautifully and joints of meat shrink less when cooked in the Slo-Cooker.

A Slo-Cooker is ideal for flexible meals. Once the cooking is completed the food can be kept safely on the Low setting for several hours without spoiling; part to be eaten immediately and part to be kept warm for latecomers. Convenience is a key factor, the Slo-Cooker is easy to use and can be operated day or night. Your evening meal can be placed in it and left all day to cook. On the other hand should you wish it to be ready for mid-day it can be cooked on High setting. A Slo-Cooker is ideal for any busy person and a boon to anyone who entertains.

Finally, slow cooking, with its gentle, moist action can be of great help when preparing food for special diets, particularly fat-free diets.

One-step Slo-Cooking

The one-step method of placing the cold ingredients in the Slo-Cooker and leaving them to cook all day, or all night, is suitable for those who can spend only a limited time on preparation.

Checkpoints for One-step Slo-Cooking

First, pre-heat the Slo-Cooker and add the liquid which must be hot.

Mix the thickening agent (flour or cornflour) with a little cold water to form a paste and stir in with the ingredients. Alternatively, coat the meat with flour before adding to the Slo-Cooker. When the thickening agent is tomato purée or condensed soup, ensure these are mixed well with the other ingredients.

When roasting brush the inside of the Slo-Cooker and the joint or bird with cooking oil.

Remember that root vegetables such as onions, potatoes, carrots etc, must be cut into small pieces ($\frac{1}{4}$ in./$\frac{1}{2}$ cm.). Those which tend to discolour, such as potatoes, should be covered with the cooking liquid to avoid browning during the heating-up period.

Always mix the ingredients well. This prevents foods (chopped bacon for instance) from sticking together. Stir soups and casseroles well before serving.

Do not leave ingredients in the Slo-Cooker overnight to be cooked the next day. If your Slo-Cooker has a removable pot, do not store the ingredients in the pot in a refrigerator before cooking.

When preparing recipes in this book by the one-step method add at least 3 hours on Low setting to the recommended cooking time. Recipes not suitable for one-step cooking are marked thus . . . . .

How to use your Slo-Cooker

Follow manufacturers' instructions carefully when connecting the Slo-Cooker to the power supply. The appliance must be earthed.

Manufacturers' instructions are the best guide if good results are to be obtained. There are however general instructions for use and certain basic rules which apply to all types of Slo-Cooker.

GENERAL METHOD OF USE

1. With lid in position, pre-heat the Slo-Cooker for about 20 minutes on the High setting while the ingredients are being prepared. This helps to boost the starting temperature.

2. Place the ingredients in the Slo-Cooker. It may be filled to within $\frac{1}{2}$–1 inch (1–2$\frac{1}{2}$ cm.) of the top of the earthenware pot.

3. Replace the lid and select the heat setting recommended in the recipe.

4. The Slo-Cooker may now be left for the remaining cooking period.

It is important that the lid remains in position throughout cooking. If it is removed the water seal around the rim is broken and a considerable time is taken to regain the heat lost. So do resist peeping!

When cooking is completed, leftover food should always be removed from the Slo-Cooker, cooled and refrigerated or frozen. Never leave uncooked food in the Slo-Cooker to be switched on later. Ingredients prepared in advance should be stored in a separate container in the refrigerator. Cooked food, normally served hot, should not be re-heated in the Slo-Cooker.

The two heat settings available on your Slo-Cooker mean that cooking times can often be adjusted to suit your lifestyle. Generally the cooking time on High is just over half that on Low. So, if a recipe in this book is meant to be cooked for 8 hours on Low and your require the finished dish earlier, cook for 5 hours on the High setting.

Cooking times can be affected by direct draughts and cold room temperatures, and these should be avoided whenever possible. In winter when the house is empty during the day, slightly longer cooking times may be necessary, especially when cooking on the Low setting. Voltage reductions in your electricity supply can also affect cooking times slightly. These uncontrollable variations usually occur during peak cooking times and during very cold weather. If a recipe is not ready at the end of the cooking period, simply replace the lid and cook for at least another hour on High.

Remember that the temperatures achieved in the Slo-Cooker are high enough to cook the food but they do not compare with even the lowest temperature of a conventional oven. Therefore, if you are adapting a recipe for the Slo-Cooker and it is normally cooked in a hot oven, this does *not* mean that it should be cooked on High in the Slo-Cooker.

Onion Soup
Eggs Florentine
Winter Vegetable Soup
Orange and Carrot Soup

SOUPS AND STARTERS

Soups are ideal for all-day gentle simmering. There is no need to worry if they cook for a few hours longer than the recommended cooking period. The result will still be delicious—perfectly cooked and tasty, the flavours from each ingredient having developed and intermingled gently for hours.

The soups included in this section can introduce a meal delicately or they can make a meal in themselves served with crusty fresh bread and cheese.

The flavour of stock and soup prepared in a Slo-Cooker is more concentrated than that of one cooked in a saucepan in the conventional method. Remember to use leftover vegetables and bones to slow cook the basis of a good soup, casserole or stew.

Adapt any of your own favourite recipes for slow cooking and appreciate the new, richer flavour. Experiment with different herbs and spices—they cannot be spoiled.

The gentle heat of the Slo-Cooker is perfect for cooking pâtés. The slow cooked pâté is firm without being tough, with a smooth texture and a delicate blend of flavours. The Slo-Cooker can also be very versatile when an oven is not available, in a bedsitter for example. For this reason Eggs Florentine has been included in this section. All you need is a cooking plate or burner.

Your freezer and slow cooked soups and starters. Soups freeze extremely well so it is a simple matter to increase quantities when cooking in your Slo-Cooker. Eat some and freeze some in suitable amounts.

Stocks can be frozen in handy blocks for adding flavour to dishes at a later date.

Pâtés are best frozen in individual serving quantities interleaved with foil or greaseproof paper and over-wrapped with foil. Then just take out as much as you need and defrost in room temperature.

CHECKPOINTS FOR SLOW COOKING SOUPS

Remember that vegetables need longer cooking than meat so they should be cut up into fairly small pieces.

Extra flavour is added to soup if meat is browned lightly in a frying pan and vegetables gently sautéed for a few minutes.

Slow cooked soups usually require less seasoning since the ingredients retain more of their own concentrated flavours.

Thickening agents: flour or cornflour may be incorporated at the start of cooking or for the final $1-1\frac{1}{2}$ hours of cooking (see the instructions on page 10). Cream, milk and egg yolks should be added during the final $\frac{1}{2}$ hour of cooking.

When adapting your own soup recipes for slow cooking, remember to use less liquid since little evaporation takes place. A good guide is to halve the quantity, then if liked, extra liquid can be added before serving.

Stock

INGREDIENTS	Imperial	Metric	American
Bones, raw or cooked	3–4 lb.	1.4–1.8 kg.	3–4 lb.
Onion, chopped	1	1	1
Carrot, chopped	1	1	1
Celery stick or stalk, chopped	1	1	1
Black peppercorns			
Salt			
Bouquet garni	1	1	1
Boiling water			

Pre-heat Slo-Cooker on High for 20 minutes. Break up the bones as small as possible to extract the most flavour. Place all ingredients in the Slo-Cooker with sufficient boiling water to cover. Cook on Low for 10–16 hours. Strain the stock. When cool skim off surface fat.

COOKING TIME
Pre-heat 20 minutes
Low 10–16 hours

TO FREEZE
Pour stock into rigid polythene containers in suitable quantities for use, cover and freeze.

CHECKPOINT
The basic method for making stock is given. Most bones can of course be replaced with a poultry carcass, skin and giblets, or fish trimmings (with a little lemon peel).

Vichyssoise

 Serves 6

INGREDIENTS	Imperial	Metric	American
Butter	2 oz.	50 g.	¼ cup
Onions, chopped	2	2	2
Clove garlic, crushed	1 small	1 small	1 small
Leeks, thinly sliced	1½ lb.	675 g.	1½ lb.
Potatoes, chopped	2	2	2
Salt and pepper			
Chicken stock	1½ pt.	900 ml.	3¾ cups
Double cream or thick cream			
Chopped chives			

Pre-heat Slo-Cooker on High for 20 minutes. Heat the butter in a large pan and sauté the onions, garlic and leeks gently for 3–4 minutes. Add the potatoes, seasoning and chicken stock. Bring to the boil then transfer to Slo-Cooker. Cook on Low for 8–10 hours. Liquidise the soup. Serve chilled. To garnish stir in a little double cream and top with chopped chives.

COOKING TIME
Pre-heat 20 minutes
Low 8–10 hours

TO FREEZE
Omit garlic, pack into rigid polythene containers, cover and freeze. Season with garlic or garlic salt at reheating stage.

Note: If you want a pure white soup then you should use only the white part of the leeks.

Potato and Leek Soup

   Serves 6

INGREDIENTS

	Imperial	Metric	American
Butter	1½ oz.	40 g.	3 tbsp.
Potatoes, thinly sliced	1 lb.	450 g.	1 lb.
Leeks, thinly sliced	1½ lb.	700 g.	1½ lb.
Chicken stock	1 pt.	600 ml.	2½ cups
Salt and pepper			
Egg Yolks, beaten	2	2	2
Milk	½ pt.	300 ml.	1¼ cups

Pre-heat Slo-Cooker on High for 20 minutes. Heat the butter in a large pan and sauté the potatoes and leeks gently for 3–4 minutes. Add the chicken stock and seasoning. Bring to the boil then transfer to Slo-Cooker. Cook on Low for 8–10 hours. 30 minutes before serving stir in the beaten egg yolks and milk and continue cooking on Low.

COOKING TIME
Pre-heat 20 minutes
Low 8–10 hours

TO FREEZE
Omit egg yolks and milk. Pack into rigid polythene container, cover and freeze. Stir in egg yolks and milk before serving. Reheat gently, without boiling.

Watercress Soup

 Serves 4–6

INGREDIENTS

	Imperial	Metric	American
Butter	2 oz.	50 g.	¼ cup
Onion, finely chopped	1	1	1
Bunches watercress	2	2	2
Chicken stock	1 pt.	600 ml.	2½ cups
Salt and pepper			
Milk	½ pt	300 ml.	1¼ cups

Pre-heat Slo-Cooker on High for 20 minutes. Heat the butter in a large pan and sauté the onion gently until transparent. Stir in the washed watercress and cook for a further 2–3 minutes, stirring all the time. Add the stock and seasoning and bring to the boil. Transfer to Slo-Cooker. Cook on Low for 6–8 hours, liquidise the soup, stir in the milk and reheat to serve. Garnish with a few watercress leaves.

COOKING TIME
Pre-heat 20 minutes
Low 6–8 hours

TO FREEZE
Omit milk. Pack liquidised soup into rigid polythene container, cover and freeze. Stir in milk on reheating.

Beef Broth

  Serves 6–8

INGREDIENTS

	Imperial	Metric	American
Cooking oil	*1 tbsp.*	*15 ml.*	*1 tbsp.*
Stewing steak, finely chopped	*8 oz.*	*225 g.*	*½ lb.*
Onions, diced	*8 oz.*	*225 g.*	*½ lb.*
Carrots, diced	*8 oz.*	*225 g.*	*½ lb.*
Potatoes, diced	*8 oz.*	*225 g.*	*½ lb.*
Leeks, thinly sliced	*1*	*1*	*1*
Flour	*1 tbsp. rounded*	*1 tbsp. rounded*	*1 tbsp. rounded*
Beef stock	*2 pt.*	*1.1 litre*	*5 cups*
Pearl barley	*1 oz.*	*25 g.*	*1 oz.*
Salt and pepper			

Pre-heat Slo-Cooker on High for 20 minutes. Heat the cooking oil in a large pan and brown the meat gently on all sides. Transfer to Slo-Cooker. In the same oil sauté the vegetables gently for 3–4 minutes. Stir in the flour then gradually add the stock, stirring well. Add barley and season well. Bring to the boil then transfer to Slo-Cooker and stir the mixture well. Cook on Low for 6–10 hours. Stir well before serving.

COOKING TIME
Pre-heat 20 minutes
Low 6–10 hours

TO FREEZE
Pack into rigid polythene container, cover and freeze.

Pea Soup

 Serves 6–8

INGREDIENTS

	Imperial	Metric	American
Split peas	*8 oz.*	*225 g.*	*½ lb.*
Bicarbonate of soda	*1 tsp.*	*1 tsp.*	*1 tsp.*
Butter	*1 oz.*	*25 g.*	*2 tbsp.*
Rashers or slices of streaky bacon, chopped	*4*	*4*	*4*
Leek, chopped	*1*	*1*	*1*
Sticks or stalks of celery chopped	*1 small*	*1 small*	*1 small*
Chicken stock	*1¾ pt.*	*1 litre*	*4½ cups*
Salt and black pepper			

Soak the peas in plenty of water with the bicarbonate of soda for 5–6 hours, or overnight.
Pre-heat Slo-Cooker on High for 20 minutes. Heat the butter in a large pan and sauté the bacon, leek and celery gently for 3–4 minutes. Stir in the drained peas and chicken stock. Season well. Bring to the boil and transfer to Slo-Cooker. Cook on Low for 8–10 hours. Liquidise or mash the soup and reheat before serving.

COOKING TIME
Pre-heat 20 minutes
Low 8–10 hours

TO FREEZE
Pack into rigid polythene container, cover and freeze.

Bortsch

 Serves 6–8

INGREDIENTS

	Imperial	Metric	American
Uncooked beetroot, skinned and grated	1 lb.	450 g.	1 lb.
Carrot, finely chopped	1 large	1 large	1 large
Onion, finely chopped	1 large	1 large	1 large
Bay leaf			
Chicken stock, boiling	2 pt.	1.1 litre	5 cups
Salt and pepper			
Juice ½ lemon			
Sour cream or natural unsweetened yoghurt	¼ pt.	150 ml.	⅔ cup
Chopped parsley			

Pre-heat Slo-Cooker on High for 20 minutes. Place the prepared vegetables in the Slo-Cooker along with the bay leaf and boiling chicken stock. Season with salt and pepper and add the lemon juice. Cook on Low for 8–10 hours. Sieve the soup. Stir in the sour cream or yoghurt and garnish with chopped parsley to serve.

COOKING TIME
Pre-heat 20 minutes
Low 8–10 hours

TO FREEZE
Omit sour cream or yoghurt. Pack into rigid polythene container, cover and freeze. Stir in the cream or yoghurt on reheating, and garnish with parsley.

CHECKPOINT
This soup may be served hot or chilled.

Minestrone

 Serves 8–10

INGREDIENTS	Imperial	Metric	American
Cooking oil	1 tbsp.	15 ml.	1 tbsp.
Butter	1 oz.	25 g.	2 tbsp.
Onion, chopped	1	1	1
Clove garlic, crushed	1	1	1
Rashers or slices of streaky bacon, chopped	3–4	3–4	3–4
Carrots, finely sliced	2	2	2
Leek, finely sliced	1	1	1
Sticks or stalks of celery, chopped	2	2	2
Cabbage, shredded	$\frac{1}{4}$ cabbage	$\frac{1}{4}$ cabbage	$\frac{1}{4}$ cabbage
Green beans, sliced	4 oz.	100 g.	$\frac{1}{4}$ lb.
Beef stock	3 pt.	1.7 litres	$7\frac{1}{2}$ cups
Tomato purée or paste	2 tbsp.	2 tbsp.	2 tbsp.
Salt & Black pepper			
Short macaroni	2 oz.	50 g.	2 oz.

Pre-heat Slo-Cooker on High for 20 minutes. Heat the oil and butter in a large pan and sauté the onion, garlic, bacon, carrots, leek and celery gently for 4–5 minutes. Add all remaining ingredients, except macaroni. Bring to the boil then transfer to Slo-Cooker. Cook on Low for 6–10 hours, adding the macaroni for the final 3–4 hours of cooking. Stir well and serve with grated Parmesan cheese.

Pre-heat 20 minutes
Low 6–10 hours

TO FREEZE

Omit garlic. Pack into rigid polythene container, cover and freeze. Add garlic at reheating stage, or season with garlic salt.

French Onion Soup

 Serves 6

INGREDIENTS

	Imperial	Metric	American
Butter	1½ oz.	40 g.	3 tbsp.
Onions, thinly sliced	1½ lb.	700 g.	1½ lb.
Chicken stock	1½ pt.	1 litre	3¾ cups
Salt			
Black pepper			
Bay leaf			

Pre-heat Slo-Cooker on High for 20 minutes. Heat the butter in a large pan and sauté the onions gently till they begin to turn golden brown. Stir in the stock, season with salt and pepper and add the bay leaf. Bring to the boil then transfer to Slo-Cooker. Cook on Low for 6–8 hours. Remove bay leaf. Serve with thick slices of crusty French bread and cheese.

COOKING TIME
Pre-heat 20 minutes
Low 6–8 hours

TO FREEZE
Pack into rigid polythene container, cover and freeze.

Celery Soup

 Serves 6

INGREDIENTS

	Imperial	Metric	American
Butter	2 oz.	50 g.	¼ cup
Celery, finely chopped	1 head	1 head	1 head
Onion, finely chopped	1 large	1 large	1 large
Water	1¾ pt.	1 litre	4½ cups
Chicken stock cubes	3	3	3
Good pinch mixed herbs			
Salt			
Black pepper			

Pre-heat Slo-Cooker on High for 20 minutes. Heat the butter in a large pan and sauté the celery and onion gently for 3–4 minutes. Add the remaining ingredients and bring to the boil. Transfer to Slo-Cooker. Cook on Low for 6–10 hours. Stir well before serving.

COOKING TIME
Pre-heat 20 minutes
Low 6–10 hours

TO FREEZE
Pack into rigid polythene container, cover and freeze.

Note: If preferred, this soup may be liquidised for a smoother consistency. To make Cream of Celery Soup, stir in ¼ pt./150 ml./⅔ cup double (thick) cream to the liquidised mixture, re-heat but do not boil.

Lentil Soup

 Serves 6

INGREDIENTS	Imperial	Metric	American
Butter	*1 oz.*	*25 g.*	*2 tbsp.*
Rashers or slices of streaky bacon, chopped	*4*	*4*	*4*
Onions, chopped	*2*	*2*	*2*
Carrots, chopped	*2–3*	*2–3*	*2–3*
Celery sticks or stalks, chopped	*2*	*2*	*2*
Water	*2 pt.*	*1.1 litre*	*5 cups*
Tomato purée or paste	*1 tbsp.*	*1 tbsp.*	*1 tbsp.*
Bouquet garni			
Lentils	*8 oz.*	*225 g.*	*½ lb.*

Pre-heat Slo-Cooker on High for 20 minutes. Heat the butter in a large pan and sauté the bacon, onions, carrots and celery gently for 3–4 minutes. Add remaining ingredients. Bring to the boil then transfer to Slo-Cooker. Cook on Low for 6–8 hours. Remove bouquet garni. Liquidise or sieve the soup and reheat to serve.

COOKING TIME
Pre-heat 20 minutes
Low 6–8 hours

TO FREEZE
Pack into rigid polythene container, cover and freeze.

Apple Curry Soup

 Serves 6

INGREDIENTS	Imperial	Metric	American
Butter	*1 oz.*	*25 g.*	*2 tbsp.*
Onion, finely chopped	*1 medium*	*1 medium*	*1 medium*
Curry powder	*2–3 tsp.*	*2–3 tsp.*	*2–3 tsp.*
Flour	*2 tbsp.*	*2 tbsp.*	*2 tbsp.*
Chicken stock	*1¾ pt.*	*1 litre*	*4½ cups*
Grated rind and juice ½ lemon			
Cooking apples, peeled, cored and chopped	*1½ lb.*	*700 g.*	*1½ lb.*
Salt			
Black pepper			
Sour cream or natural unsweetened yoghurt	*¼ pt.*	*150 ml.*	*⅔ cup*

Pre-heat Slo-Cooker on High for 20 minutes. Heat the butter in a large pan and sauté the onion gently till transparent. Stir in the curry powder and flour. Gradually add the chicken stock, stirring all the time. Add lemon rind and juice and apples and season well. Bring to the boil and transfer to Slo-Cooker. Cook on Low for 6–8 hours. Liquidise the soup, reheat and stir in the cream or yoghurt to serve. Garnish with a few thin slices of raw apple if liked.

COOKING TIME
Pre-heat 20 minutes   Low 6–8 hours

TO FREEZE
Omit cream or yoghurt. Pack into rigid polythene container, cover and freeze. Add cream or yoghurt on reheating.

Tomato Soup

  Serves 6–8

INGREDIENTS	Imperial	Metric	American
Butter	1 oz.	25 g.	2 tbsp.
Onion, finely chopped	1	1	1
Carrot, finely chopped	1	1	1
Sticks or stalks of celery, finely chopped	2	2	2
Rashers or slices of streaky bacon, chopped	4	4	4
Tomatoes, skinned	1½ lb.	700 g.	1½ lb.
Chicken or onion stock	1½ pt.	900 ml.	3¾ cups
Sugar	1 tsp.	1 tsp.	1 tsp.
Good pinch mixed herbs			
Salt and pepper			

Pre-heat Slo-Cooker on High for 20 minutes. Heat the butter in a large pan and sauté the onion, carrot, celery and bacon gently for 3–4 minutes. Stir in the remaining ingredients, bring to the boil, then transfer to Slo-Cooker. Cook on Low for 8–10 hours. Stir well before serving.

COOKING TIME
Pre-heat 20 minutes   Low 8–10 hours.

TO FREEZE
Pack into rigid polythene container, cover and freeze.

Note: if preferred, this soup may be liquidised for a smoother consistency. To make Cream of Tomato Soup, stir in ¼ pt./150 ml./⅔ cup double cream to the liquidised mixture. Reheat (without boiling) to serve.

Spinach and Celery Soup

  Serves 6

INGREDIENTS	Imperial	Metric	American
Butter	1 oz.	25 g.	2 tbsp.
Celery, chopped	1 small head	1 small head	1 small head
Onion, chopped	1	1	1
Spinach, roughly chopped	1 lb.	450 g.	1 lb.
Water	1½ pt.	900 ml.	3¾ cup
Salt			
Freshly ground black pepper			
Milk	¼ pt.	150 ml.	⅔ cup
Double cream or thick cream			

Pre-heat Slo-Cooker on High for 20 minutes. Heat the butter in a large pan and sauté the celery and onions, gently for a few minutes. Add the spinach, water, salt and pepper and bring to the boil. Transfer to Slo-Cooker. Cook on Low for 6–10 hours. Liquidise the soup, stir in the milk, reheat and serve with a swirl of double cream.

COOKING TIME
Pre-heat 20 minutes
Low 6–10 hours

TO FREEZE
Omit milk, pack into rigid polythene container, cover and freeze. Add milk at reheating stage.

Orange and Carrot Soup

 Serves 6

INGREDIENTS

	Imperial	Metric	American
Butter	1½ oz.	40 g.	3 tbsp.
Onion, chopped	1 small	1 small	1 small
Sticks or stalks of celery	1	1	1
Carrots, finely chopped	1 lb.	450 g.	1 lb.
Cornflour or cornstarch	3 tbsp.	3 tbsp.	3 tbsp.
Water	1¼ pt.	700 ml.	3¼ cups
Onion stock cubes	2	2	2
Rind and juice of oranges	4	4	4
Salt and pepper			
Bouquet garni			

Pre-heat Slo-Cooker on High for 20 minutes. Heat the butter in a large pan and sauté the onion, celery and carrots gently for about 5 minutes. Stir in the cornflour then gradually add the water, stirring continuously. Add the remaining ingredients and bring to the boil. Transfer to Slo-Cooker. Cook on Low for 8–10 hours. Remove bouquet garni. Serve with crusty fresh bread.

COOKING TIME
Pre-heat 20 minutes
Low 8–10 hours

TO FREEZE
Pack in rigid polythene container, cover and freeze.

Note: to obtain a smoother consistency, this soup may be liquidised.

Cucumber and Mint Soup

 Serves 6

INGREDIENTS

	Imperial	Metric	American
Butter	1 oz.	25 g.	2 tbsp.
Onion, chopped	1	1	1
Cucumber, peeled and sliced	1 large	1 large	1 large
Chicken stock	1 pt.	600 ml.	2½ cups
Mint, chopped fresh or	2 tbsp.	2 tbsp.	2 tbsp.
Dried mint	1 tbsp.	1 tbsp.	1 tbsp.
Salt and pepper			
Milk	½ pt.	300 ml.	1¼ cups
Carton natural unsweetened yoghurt	1 small	1 small	1 small

Pre-heat Slo-Cooker on High for 20 minutes. In a large pan heat the butter and sauté the onion until transparent. Stir in the cucumber, chicken stock, mint and seasoning and bring to the boil. Transfer to Slo-Cooker. Cook on Low for 4–8 hours. Liquidise the soup, stir in the milk and chill. Serve in chilled bowls with a little yoghurt stirred in each.

COOKING TIME
Pre-heat 20 minutes
Low 4–8 hours

TO FREEZE
Omit milk, pour into rigid polythene container, cover and freeze.

Note: This soup may also be served hot with croutons.

Winter Vegetable Soup

  Serves 6

INGREDIENTS

	Imperial	Metric	American
Butter	2 oz.	50 g.	$\frac{1}{4}$ cup
Onions, chopped	8 oz.	225 g.	$\frac{1}{2}$ lb.
Carrots, diced	8 oz.	225 g.	$\frac{1}{2}$ lb.
Parsnips, diced	8 oz.	225 g.	$\frac{1}{2}$ lb.
Celery sticks or stalks, chopped	2	2	2
Tomatoes, skinned and chopped	8 oz.	225 g.	$\frac{1}{2}$ lb.
Flour	3 tbsp.	3 tbsp.	3 tbsp.
Stock	$1\frac{1}{2}$ pt.	1 litre	$3\frac{3}{4}$ cup
Bouquet garni			
Salt and pepper			

Pre-heat Slo-Cooker on High for 20 minutes. Heat the butter in a large pan and sauté the onions, carrots, parsnips and celery gently for about 5 minutes. Stir in the tomatoes. Mix the flour with a little cold stock to form a smooth paste then add this, the remaining stock and bouquet garni to the mixture. Season well. Bring to the boil and transfer to Slo-Cooker. Cook on Low for 6–10 hours. Remove bouquet garni. Serve with baked potatoes and cheese to make a filling meal.

COOKING TIME
Pre-heat 20 minutes
Low 6–10 hours

CHECKPOINT
This soup may be made using other selections of winter vegetables. Use your favourite herbs to add interest replacing the bouquet garni.

Farmhouse Pâté

  Serves 8–10

INGREDIENTS

	Imperial	Metric	American
Lamb's liver, chopped	8 oz.	225 g.	$\frac{1}{2}$ lb.
Chicken liver, chopped	8 oz.	225 g.	$\frac{1}{2}$ lb.
Streaky bacon, chopped	4 oz.	100 g.	$\frac{1}{4}$ lb.
Onion, chopped	1 small	1 small	1 small
Clove garlic, crushed	1	1	1
Eggs	2	2	2
Milk	$\frac{1}{4}$ pt.	150 ml.	$\frac{2}{3}$ cup
Salt	1 tsp.	1 tsp.	1 tsp.
Black pepper			

Pre-heat Slo-Cooker on High for 20 minutes. Place all ingredients into a powerful blender and blend till smooth (it may be necessary to do this in portions). Pour into an ovenproof container and cover with buttered foil. Stand the container in the Slo-Cooker and pour boiling water round, to come nearly to the top of the dish. Cook on Low for 6–8 hours. Remove the pâté from the Slo-Cooker and allow to cool in the container before turning out. Garnish with lettuce and thin slices of cucumber and tomato.

COOKING TIME
Pre-heat 20 minutes
Low 6–8 hours

CHECKPOINT
The ovenproof container used should fit neatly into the Slo-Cooker without touching the sides or lid. It may be necessary to fit a string handle to the container to enable easy removal when hot.

Canneloni

 Serves 4

INGREDIENTS

	Imperial	Metric	American
Canneloni	8 oz.	225 g.	$\frac{1}{2}$ lb.
Stuffing :			
Lean bacon, chopped	8 oz.	225 g.	$\frac{1}{2}$ lb.
Fresh breadcrumbs	4 oz.	100 g.	2 cups
Cheese, grated	4 oz.	100 g.	$\frac{1}{4}$ lb.
Salt and pepper			
Egg, beaten	1	1	1
Sauce :			
Butter	$\frac{1}{2}$ oz.	15 g.	1 tbsp.
Onion, finely chopped	1 small	1 small	1 small
Flour	2 tbsp.	2 tbsp.	2 tbsp.
Stock	$\frac{1}{2}$ pt.	300 ml.	$1\frac{1}{4}$ cup
Tomatoes, canned	14 oz.	397 g.	1 lb.
Mixed herbs	gd. pinch	gd. pinch	gd. pinch
Salt and pepper			

Butter inside the Slo-Cooker; pre-heat on High for 20 minutes. Bind the dry stuffing ingredients with egg. Fill the pasta tubes with this mixture. To prepare the sauce, heat the butter in a saucepan and sauté the onion gently until transparent. Stir in flour, add the stock gradually, then the tomatoes and herbs. Season well. Bring to the boil, stirring continuously. Arrange the stuffed pasta tubes in the Slo-Cooker and pour the sauce over, making sure it covers the pasta. Cook on Low for 6–8 hours.

COOKING TIME

Pre-heat 20 minutes
Low 6–8 hours.

TO FREEZE

Arrange the canneloni on a foil tray and pour the sauce over. Cover and freeze.

CHECKPOINT

For best results use quick-cook pasta.

Gourmet Pâté

 Serves 10

INGREDIENTS	Imperial	Metric	American
Bay leaves	4	4	4
Streaky bacon rashers or slices	4	4	4
Chicken liver	1 lb.	450 g.	1 lb.
Onion, chopped	1 medium	1 medium	1 medium
Clove garlic	1	1	1
Dry mustard	1 tsp.	1 tsp.	1 tsp.
Mixed herbs	½ tsp.	½ tsp.	½ tsp.
Black pepper and salt			
Brandy (optional)	2 tbsp.	30 ml.	2 tbsp.
Flour	3 oz	75 g.	¾ cup
Butter	3 oz.	75 g.	⅓ cup
Milk	½ pt.	300 ml.	1¼ cup

Pre-heat Slo-Cooker on High for 20 minutes. Arrange the bay leaves in the base of an ovenproof container then lay the bacon rashers on top (base only). Place the chicken liver, onion, garlic, mustard, mixed herbs, seasoning and brandy (optional) into a powerful blender and blend till smooth (it may be necessary to do this in portions). Heat the butter in a saucepan and stir in the flour. Cook for a further few minutes then gradually add the milk, stirring well. Bring to the boil, stirring continuously. Mix together the liver and sauce and stir well. Pour the mixture into the prepared ovenproof container and cover with buttered foil. Stand the container in the Slo-Cooker and pour boiling water round to come nearly to the top of the dish. Cook on Low for 6–8 hours. Remove the pâté from the Slo-Cooker and allow to cool in the container before turning out onto a bed of lettuce.

COOKING TIME
Pre-heat 20 minutes
Low 6–8 hours

TO FREEZE
Pâté is best frozen in slices, interleaved with paper. Wrap in foil and freeze. Take slices out of the freezer as required.

CHECKPOINT
The ovenproof container used should fit neatly into the Slo-Cooker without touching the sides or lid. Fit it with a string handle to enable easy removal when hot.

Eggs Florentine

 Serves 4

INGREDIENTS	Imperial	Metric	American
Butter	1 oz.	25 g.	2 tbsp.
Spinach, washed and roughly chopped	1 lb.	450 g.	1 lb.
Eggs	4	4	4
Sauce :			
Butter	1 oz.	25 g.	2 tbsp.
Flour	1 oz.	25 g.	$\frac{1}{4}$ cup
Milk	$\frac{1}{2}$ pt.	300 ml.	$1\frac{1}{4}$ cup
Salt and pepper			
Cheese, finely grated			

Butter the inside of the Slo-Cooker and pre-heat on High for 20 minutes. Arrange the roughly chopped spinach in the Slo-Cooker and cook on High for 1 hour.

To make sauce : Heat the butter in a saucepan and stir in the flour. Cook gently for 2–3 minutes. Gradually add the milk, stirring continuously, and bring to the boil. Season well. Use the base of a cup to make four depressions in the spinach. Break one egg into each. Pour the prepared sauce over, then cook on High for a further 2 hours. Sprinkle with a little grated cheese to serve.

COOKING TIME
Pre-heat 20 minutes
High 1 hour and 2 hours

CHECKPOINT
If frozen spinach is used, allow to thaw and omit first cooking stage (i.e. total cooking time 2 hours on High).

SAUCES

Sauce-making can prove a time-consuming affair. Your Slo-Cooker, however, can take much of the effort out of this chore. Your Slo-Cooker can be used to prepare those sauces which often form the important ingredient in a dish. Final additions can then be made at the last minute.

At the end of the cooking period you may like to use your blender to make a perfectly smooth sauce.

I have given seven sauces to try in the following pages and hope these will encourage you to experiment with others.

YOUR FREEZER AND SLOW COOKED SAUCES

Here is the ideal opportunity to stock up the freezer with suitable amounts of delicious sauces ready to add interest to the simplest meal at a moment's notice.

CHECKPOINTS FOR SLOW COOKING SAUCES

Extra flavour is added to the sauce if meats are browned lightly and vegetables sautéed gently before slow cooking.

Sauce prepared in the Slo-Cooker requires less seasoning than one cooked conventionally, since the ingredients retain more of their own concentrated flavours.

Cut up vegetables into small even-sized pieces to ensure even cooking.

Thickening agents: flour and cornflour can be added at the start of the cooking period; cream, milk and egg yolks should be added during the final $\frac{1}{2}$ hour.

When adapting your own sauce recipes for slow cooking remember to use less liquid since it does not evaporate as it would if cooked conventionally in a saucepan. A little extra liquid to thin the sauce can always be added before serving.

Espagnole Sauce
Curry Sauce
Tomato Sauce
Mushroom Sauce

Espagnole Sauce

  Serves 6–8

INGREDIENTS	Imperial	Metric	American
Butter	*2 oz.*	*50 g.*	*¼ cup*
Streaky bacon rashers or slices, finely chopped	*2*	*2*	*2*
Onion, finely chopped	*1*	*1*	*1*
Carrot, finely chopped	*1*	*1*	*1*
Mushrooms, finely chopped	*2 oz.*	*50 g.*	*2 oz.*
Flour	*4 tbsp.*	*4 tbsp.*	*4 tbsp.*
Beef stock	*1¼ pt.*	*750 ml.*	*3¼ cup*
Tomato purée or paste	*4 tbsp.*	*4 tbsp.*	*4 tbsp.*
Bouquet garni			
Salt and pepper			

Pre-heat Slo-Cooker on High for 20 minutes. Heat the butter in a saucepan and sauté the bacon, onion, carrot and mushrooms gently for 3–4 minutes. Stir in the flour. Gradually add the stock, stirring all the time, then the remaining ingredients. Bring to the boil and transfer to Slo-Cooker. Cook on Low for 5–7 hours.

COOKING TIME
Pre-heat 20 minutes
Low 5–7 hours

TO FREEZE
Pack into rigid polythene containers in suitable serving quantities, cover and freeze.

Curry Sauce

  Serves 6–8

INGREDIENTS	Imperial	Metric	American
Cooking oil	*2 tbsp.*	*30 ml.*	*2 tbsp.*
Onions, finely chopped	*1 lb.*	*450 g.*	*1 lb.*
Curry powder	*1½–2 tbsp.*	*1½–2 tbsp.*	*1½–2 tbsp.*
Cumin	*1 tsp.*	*1 tsp.*	*1 tsp.*
Flour	*3 tbsp.*	*3 tbsp.*	*3 tbsp.*
Can tomatoes	*8 oz.*	*226 g.*	*½ lb.*
Stock	*1 pt.*	*600 ml.*	*2½ cups*
Vinegar or lemon juice	*2 tbsp.*	*30 ml.*	*2 tbsp.*
Chutney	*1 rounded tbsp.*	*1 rounded tbsp.*	*1 rounded tbsp.*
Bay leaf			
Salt and pepper			

Pre-heat Slo-Cooker on High for 20 minutes. Heat the cooking oil in a saucepan and sauté the onions, curry powder and cumin gently for 4–5 minutes. Stir in the flour then add the tomatoes, stirring well. Add remaining ingredients, bring to the boil and transfer to Slo-Cooker. Cook on Low for 6–8 hours.

COOKING TIME
Pre-heat 20 minutes
Low 6–8 hours

TO FREEZE
Pack in suitable amounts in rigid polythene containers, cover and freeze.

Bolognese Sauce

  Serves 6

INGREDIENTS

	Imperial	Metric	American
Cooking oil	1 tbsp.	15 ml.	1 tbsp.
Onions, finely chopped	2	2	2
Clove garlic, crushed	1	1	1
Raw minced beef	1½ lb.	700 g.	1½ lb.
Mushrooms, chopped	4 oz.	100 g.	¼ lb.
Can tomatoes	15 oz.	425 g.	1 lb.
Oregano	2 tsp.	2 tsp.	2 tsp.
Beef stock	½ pt.	300 ml.	1¼ cup
Tomato purée or paste	2 tbsp.	2 tbsp.	2 tbsp.
Salt and pepper			

Pre-heat Slo-Cooker on High for 20 minutes. Heat the cooking oil in a large pan and sauté the onions and garlic gently until transparent. Remove. In the same pan brown the minced beef lightly for about 5 minutes. Stir in the onions and garlic and remaining ingredients, seasoning to taste. Bring to the boil and transfer to Slo-Cooker. Cook on High for 30 minutes then switch to Low for 6–8 hours. Stir well before serving with boiled spaghetti and grated Parmesan cheese.

COOKING TIME
Pre-heat 20 minutes
High 30 minutes
Low 6–8 hours

TO FREEZE
Omit garlic and oregano. Pack into rigid polythene container, cover and freeze. Add garlic (or garlic salt) and oregano on reheating.

Sweet-Sour Sauce

  Serves 4–6

INGREDIENTS	Imperial	Metric	American
Cooking oil	1 tbsp.	15 ml.	1 tbsp.
Onion, finely chopped	1	1	1
Clove garlic, crushed	1	1	1
Cornflour or cornstarch	2 tbsp.	2 tbsp.	2 tbsp.
Sherry	$\frac{1}{4}$ pt.	150 ml.	$\frac{2}{3}$ cup
Soy sauce	4 tbsp.	60 ml.	4 tbsp.
Vinegar	2 tbsp.	30 ml.	2 tbsp.
Onion stock	$\frac{1}{2}$ pt.	300 ml.	$1\frac{1}{4}$ cup
Can crushed pineapple	$8\frac{1}{2}$ oz.	240 g.	$\frac{1}{2}$ lb.
Brown sugar	2 tbsp.	2 tbsp.	2 tbsp.

Pre-heat Slo-Cooker on High for 20 minutes. Heat the cooking oil in a saucepan and sauté the onion and garlic gently until transparent. Stir in the cornflour. Gradually add the remaining ingredients, stirring well. Bring to the boil then transfer to Slo-Cooker. Cook on Low for 4–6 hours.

COOKING TIME
Pre-heat 20 minutes
Low 4–6 hours

TO FREEZE
Pack into rigid polythene container, cover and freeze.

Mushroom Sauce

 Serves 6–8

INGREDIENTS

	Imperial	Metric	American
Butter	1 oz.	25 g.	2 tbsp.
Cooking oil	2 tbsp.	2 tbsp.	2 tbsp.
Onion, finely chopped	1	1	1
Beef stock	½ pt.	300 ml.	1¼ cup
Mushrooms, sliced	1½ lb.	700 g.	1½ lb.
Cornflour or cornstarch	2 tbsp.	2 tbsp.	2 tbsp.
Worcestershire sauce	2 tbsp.	2 tbsp.	2 tbsp.
Tomato purée	2 tbsp.	2 tbsp.	2 tbsp.
Beef stock	½ pt.	300 ml.	1¼ cup
Oregano	2 tsp.	2 tsp.	2 tsp.
Salt			
Black pepper			

Pre-heat Slo-Cooker on High for 20 minutes. Heat the butter and cooking oil in a large pan and sauté the onions gently until transparent. Stir in the cornflour. Gradually add the beef stock, stirring all the time, then all remaining ingredients. Bring to the boil, stirring well. Transfer to Slo-Cooker. Cook on low for 4–8 hours. Stir well before serving.

COOKING TIME
Pre-heat 20 minutes
Low 4–8 hours

TO FREEZE
Pack in rigid polythene containers in suitable serving portions, cover and freeze.

Tomato Sauce

 Serves 6–8

INGREDIENTS

	Imperial	Metric	American
Butter	1 oz.	25 g.	2 tbsp.
Onion, finely chopped	1	1	1
Carrot, finely chopped	1	1	1
Celery stick or stalk, finely chopped	1	1	1
Streaky bacon rashers or slices, chopped	4	4	4
Flour	2 tbsp.	2 tbsp.	2 tbsp.
Chicken stock	1 pt.	600 ml.	2½ cup
Tomatoes, skinned and sliced	1 lb.	450 g.	1 lb.
Juice ½ lemon			
Sugar	1 tsp.	1 tsp.	1 tsp.
Bay leaves	2	2	2
Ground cloves	1 pinch	1 pinch	1 pinch
Salt			
Black pepper			

Pre-heat Slo-Cooker on High for 20 minutes. Heat the butter in a large pan and sauté the onion, carrot, celery and bacon gently for 3–4 minutes. Stir in the flour. Gradually add the chicken stock, stirring continuously. Add remaining ingredients, bring to the boil, then transfer to Slo-Cooker. Cook on Low for 8–10 hours. Remove the bay leaves before liquidising or sieving the sauce. Reheat to serve.

COOKING TIME
Pre-heat 20 minutes
Low 8–10 hours

TO FREEZE
Pack in rigid polythene containers in suitable serving quantities, cover and freeze.

Sauce Bordelaise

  Serves 4–6

INGREDIENTS	Imperial	Metric	American
Butter	2 oz.	50 g.	$\frac{1}{4}$ cup
Onion, finely chopped	1 large	1 large	1 large
Clove garlic, crushed	1	1	1
Flour	3 tbsp.	3 tbsp.	3 tbsp.
Beef stock	$\frac{1}{2}$ pt.	300 ml.	$1\frac{1}{4}$ cup
Red wine	$\frac{1}{2}$ pt.	300 ml.	$1\frac{1}{4}$ cup
Salt and pepper			

Pre-heat Slo-Cooker on High for 20 minutes. Heat the butter in a saucepan and sauté the onion and garlic gently until transparent. Stir in the flour then gradually add the stock and wine, stirring continuously. Season with salt and pepper. Bring to the boil and transfer to Slo-Cooker. Cook on Low for 6–8 hours. Stir well before serving.

COOKING TIME
Pre-heat 20 minutes
Low 6–8 hours

TO FREEZE
Pack into rigid polythene container, cover and freeze.

Fish

Fish cooked in the Slo-Cooker retains every bit of its delicate flavour. Though it is not suitable for all-day cooking I am sure you will wish to try it. Once tasted, slow cooked fish is not forgotten.

Another advantage of preparing fish in the Slo-Cooker is that it remains beautifully whole. The moist heat is so gentle that whole fish or fish pieces do not disintegrate. Treat yourself to Almond Trout and appreciate what I mean.

Slow cooking also takes away the exact timing normally necessary with fish cookery, though timing is of course more crucial than, say, slow cooking soups or meat.

By using the minimum amount of liquid to cook the fish and by using the cooking liquor to form a sauce, no flavour is discarded.

I hope you enjoy the following recipes. Do remember that where a white fish is included in a recipe, for example, it will taste just as good if replaced with another (perhaps a family favourite or a less expensive variety).

YOUR FREEZER AND SLOW COOKED FISH

If fish is to be appreciated at its best, it should be eaten as soon as it is cooked. I therefore do not consider it worthwhile freezing any of the recipes in the next few pages.

Frozen fish should be thawed before slow cooking.

CHECKPOINTS FOR SLOW COOKING FISH

Prepare the fish in the usual way—clean, trim, wash and season.

Cooking time will depend on the type of fish and its preparation (whole, fillets, steaks or cubes). When in doubt consult a similar recipe in this chapter or in your manufacturer's instruction book.

Do not attempt to put too many whole fish in the Slo-Cooker or the weight of the top ones could affect the finished appearance and texture of those at the bottom. Four is an ideal quantity.

Liquids used may be stock, water, wine, cider or fruit juice. Use small quantities only to retain the most fish flavour.

Thickening agents such as flour and cornflour are best added to casserole-type dishes before slow cooking. Use the method given in the recipes that follow. Where a sauce is to accompany whole fish you may prefer to thicken after cooking. Place the cooked fish on a serving dish and keep warm, then transfer the cooking liquor to a saucepan for speedy thickening with flour, cornflour, cream etc.

Cream, milk and egg yolks should be added to the Slo-Cooker during the final $\frac{1}{2}$ hour of the cooking period.

When adapting your own recipes for slow cooking consult the recipes that follow for guidance. Remember you will probably need less liquid—you can always add a little extra just before serving.

Fish Bake

 Serves 4

INGREDIENTS	Imperial	Metric	American
Butter	1 oz.	25 g.	2 tbsp.
Onion, finely chopped	1	1	1
Mackerel fillets, skinned and cubed	1 lb.	450 g.	1 lb.
Cod fillets, skinned and cubed	1 lb.	450 g.	1 lb.
Button mushrooms, sliced	4 oz.	100 g.	$\frac{1}{4}$ lb.
Tomatoes, skinned and sliced	8 oz.	225 g.	$\frac{1}{2}$ lb.
Juice 1 lemon			
Salt			
Black pepper			
Water	2–3 tbsp.	2–3 tbsp.	2–3 tbsp.

Pre-heat Slo-Cooker on High for 20 minutes. Heat the butter in a large pan and sauté the onion gently until transparent. Stir in the remaining ingredients, bring to the boil and transfer to Slo-Cooker. Cook on Low for 2–4 hours. Serve with triangles of fried bread.

COOKING TIME
Pre-heat 20 minutes
Low 2–4 hours

Note: If your Slo-Cooker has a removable pot a topping of creamed or sliced potatoes can be added and crisped in the oven or under a hot grill.

Fish Casserole

 Serves 4

INGREDIENTS	Imperial	Metric	American
White fish, such as cod or haddock, cut into cubes	$1\frac{1}{4}$ lb.	675 g.	$1\frac{1}{4}$ lb.
Cornflour or cornstarch	1 tbsp.	1 tbsp.	1 tbsp.
Cooking oil	1 tbsp.	15 ml.	1 tbsp.
Onion, finely chopped	1	1	1
Courgettes, thinly sliced	8 oz.	225 g.	$\frac{1}{2}$ lb.
Dry white wine or cider	$\frac{1}{2}$ pt.	300 ml.	$1\frac{1}{4}$ cups
Bay leaf			
Bouquet garni			

Pre-heat Slo-Cooker on High for 20 minutes. Coat the fish with the cornflour. Heat the cooking oil in a large pan and sauté the onion and courgettes gently for 4–5 minutes. Add the wine/cider, bay leaf and bouquet garni and stir in the fish. Bring to the boil and transfer to Slo-Cooker. Cook on Low for 3–6 hours.

Remove bay leaf and bouquet garni before serving.

COOKING TIME
Pre-heat 20 minutes
Low 3–6 hours

Curried Haddock

 Serves 4

INGREDIENTS	Imperial	Metric	American
Haddock, skinned and cubed	1¼ lbs.	675 g.	1¼ lbs.
Cornflour or cornstarch, seasoned	1 tbsp.	1 tbsp.	1 tbsp.
Cooking oil	1 tbsp.	1 tbsp.	1 tbsp.
Onion, finely chopped	1 large	1 large	1 large
Curry powder	3 tsp.	3 tsp.	3 tsp.
Chilli powder	½ tsp.	½ tsp.	½ tsp.
Water	½ pt.	300 ml.	1¼ cup
Juice 1 lemon			
Sultanas	2 tbsp.	2 tbsp.	2 tbsp.
Bay leaf			
Salt and pepper			

Pre-heat Slo-Cooker on High for 20 minutes. Coat the haddock cubes with the seasoned cornflour. In a large pan heat the cooking oil and sauté the onion, curry powder and chilli powder gently for 5 minutes. Stir in the haddock then carefully stir in the water. Add the remaining ingredients, bring to the boil, and transfer to Slo-Cooker. Cook on Low for 2–4 hours.

COOKING TIME
Pre-heat 20 minutes
Low 2–4 hours

Haddock and Eggs

 Serves 4

INGREDIENTS	Imperial	Metric	American
Butter	1 oz.	25 g.	2 tbsp.
Smoked haddock cut into 4 pieces	1½ lb.	700 g.	1½ lb.
Pepper			
Milk and water			
Eggs	4	4	4

Butter the inside of the Slo-Cooker and pre-heat on High for 20 minutes.

Arrange the haddock pieces in the Slo-Cooker and pour over sufficient milk and water (equal quantities) to just cover. Season with pepper. Cook on Low for 2 hours. Crack the eggs over the fish and continue to cook on Low for 1 further hour. Serve immediately.

COOKING TIME
Pre-heat 20 minutes
Low 2 hours + 1 hour

Stuffed Plaice with Orange

 Serves 4

INGREDIENTS	Imperial	Metric	American
Margarine	½ oz.	15 g.	1 tbsp.
Mushrooms, chopped	4 oz.	100 g.	¼ lb.
Hard-boiled eggs, chopped	2	2	2
Salt and pepper			
Small plaice fillets, skinned	8	8	8
Butter	1 oz.	25 g.	2 tbsp.
Juice of oranges	2	2	2

Pre-heat Slo-Cooker on High for 20 minutes.
Heat the margarine in a saucepan and gently sauté the mushrooms for 1–2 minutes. Stir in the eggs and seasoning. Place a little of the mixture on the skinned side of each fillet. Roll up and secure with cotton or a wooden cocktail stick. Arrange the fish in the Slo-Cooker, dot with the butter and pour round the orange juice. Cook on Low for 2½–3 hours. If liked, the sauce may be thickened with cornflour before serving.

COOKING TIME
Pre-heat 20 minutes
Low 2½–3 hours

Portuguese Skate

 Serves 4

INGREDIENTS

	Imperial	Metric	American
Skate (4 pieces)	1½–2 lb.	700 g.–1 kg.	1½–2 lb.
Butter	1 oz.	25 g.	2 tbsp.
Onion, finely chopped	1 medium	1 medium	1 medium
Large tomatoes, skinned and sliced	4	4	4
Tomato purée or paste	4 tbsp.	4 tbsp.	4 tbsp.
Few stuffed olives, sliced			
Salt and pepper			

Butter the base of the Slo-Cooker and pre-heat on High for 20 minutes. Heat the butter in a saucepan and sauté the onion gently till transparent. Stir in the tomatoes, tomato purée, olives and season to taste. Bring to the boil. Season the skate pieces with salt and pepper and arrange in the base of the Slo-Cooker. Pour the sauce over. Cook on Low for 2½–4 hours.

COOKING TIME
Pre-heat 20 minutes
Low 2½–4 hours

Herrings with Gooseberries

 Serves 4–6

INGREDIENTS	Imperial	Metric	American
Butter	½ oz.	15 g.	1 tbsp.
Boned herrings	1 lb.	450 g.	1 lb.
Salt			
Black pepper			
Gooseberries, trimmed	8 oz.	225 g.	½ lb.
Water	4–5 tbsp.	4–5 tbsp.	4–5 tbsp.
Sugar	2 tbsp.	2 tbsp.	2 tbsp.

Butter the base of the Slo-Cooker and pre-heat on High for 20 minutes. Season the inside of the herrings with salt and pepper. Arrange the gooseberries in the Slo-Cooker, sprinkle with sugar and pour on the water. Lay the seasoned herrings on top. Cook on Low for 2–3 hours.

COOKING TIME
Pre-heat 20 minutes
Low 2–3 hours

Note: herrings may be replaced with small mackerel in this recipe.

Lemon Plaice

 Serves 4

INGREDIENTS	Imperial	Metric	American
Butter	½ oz.	15 g.	1 tbsp.
Plaice fillets, skinned	8	8	8
Salt and pepper			
Chopped chives	1 tbsp.	1 tbsp.	1 tbsp.
Cornflour	2 tsp.	2 tsp.	2 tsp.
Water	¼ pt.	150 ml.	⅔ cup
Grated rind and juice 1 lemon			
Bay leaf			

Butter the base of the Slo-Cooker then pre-heat on High for 20 minutes. Season both sides of the plaice fillets with salt and pepper. Sprinkle the chives over the cut side of the fish then roll up each fillet (chives inside). Arrange the plaice rolls in the Slo-Cooker. Mix the cornflour with a little of the water to form a smooth paste. Gradually stir in the remaining ingredients and pour the mixture round the fish. Extra seasoning may be needed. Cook on Low for 2–3 hours. Serve as a starter or with salad or vegetables as a main course.

COOKING TIME
Pre-heat 20 minutes
Low 2–3 hours

Prawn Rissotto

 Serves 4

INGREDIENTS

	Imperial	Metric	American
Cooking oil	1 tbsp.	15 ml.	1 tbsp.
Onions, finely chopped	2	2	2
Chicken stock	1½ pt.	900 ml.	3¾ cups
Button mushrooms, sliced	8 oz.	225 g.	½ lb.
Green pepper, de-seeded and chopped	1	1	1
Tomatoes, skinned and sliced	2	2	2
Easy-cook long grain rice	6 oz.	175 g.	1 cup, generous
Prawns	8 oz.	225 g.	½ lb.

Pre-heat Slo-Cooker on High for 20 minutes. Heat the cooking oil in a large pan and sauté the onions gently until transparent. Add the chicken stock, mushrooms and green pepper. Bring to the boil then transfer to Slo-Cooker. Stir in the tomatoes, rice and prawns. Cook on Low for 3–4 hours. Stir and serve immediately, adjusting seasoning if necessary.

COOKING TIME
Pre-heat 20 minutes
Low 3–4 hours

Rollmop Herrings

 Serves 4

INGREDIENTS

	Imperial	Metric	American
Herrings, cleaned and boned	6–8	6–8	6–8
Malt vinegar	¼ pt.	150 ml.	⅔ cup
Water	¼ pt.	150 ml.	⅔ cup
Onion, finely sliced	1 small	1 small	1 small
Bay leaves	2	2	2
Mace	1 blade	1 blade	1 blade
Black peppercorns	6	6	6
Salt and pepper			

Pre-heat Slo-Cooker on High for 20 minutes. Scale and clean the herrings, removing heads and tails. Season lightly on the fleshy side with salt and pepper. Roll up from the tail end, skin side outside. Mix together the remaining ingredients in a saucepan and season with salt and pepper. Bring to the boil. Arrange the herring rolls in the Slo-Cooker and pour the liquid round. Cook on Low for 4–6 hours. Arrange the herrings in a serving dish and pour the liquor over.

COOKING TIME
Pre-heat 20 minutes
Low 4–6 hours

CHECKPOINT
This dish may be served cold and as a starter, or cold or hot as a main dish with salad or boiled potatoes.

Note: boned mackerel or pilchards may also be prepared this way.

MEAT

Your Slo-Cooker could almost have been designed specifically for cooking meat; both joints and casseroles. The recipe can be left to cook all day (and part of the evening too, if necessary) without the risk of burning or overcooking, and without the worry of checking, basting, turning or stirring. And the slow, gentle heat action tenderizes even the toughest cuts of meat.

Old-fashioned flavours of the dishes 'Grandma used to make' can be recaptured in the Slo-Cooker. Use it to prepare more exotic, delicate recipes suitable for entertaining, as well as for the tasty casseroles, stews and roasts.

Whenever possible use the juices that surround the meat as part of the meal—in the form of a rich sauce for example. This way, every drop of concentrated flavour is appreciated.

You will find that slow cooked joints of meat shrink much less than those roasted conventionally—a considerable bonus when budgeting for family meals.

YOUR FREEZER AND SLOW COOKED MEATS

The majority of slow cooked meat recipes may be frozen successfully. Specific instructions are provided in the following recipes where freezing is recommended.

Frozen meat should always be thawed completely before slow cooking. Remember though that partially frozen meat is easy to handle when chopping and slicing.

CHECKPOINTS FOR SLOW COOKING MEATS

Trim excess fat from meat.

To improve the flavour, and appearance, lightly brown the meat in a separate pan before slow cooking.

Vegetables tend to need longer cooking than meat so cut them into small pieces and ensure they are immersed in the cooking liquid.

When adapting your own recipes for slow cooking reduce the quantity of liquid by approximately half. The consistency can be adjusted if necessary before serving.

Liquids may be stock, water, wine, cider, beer or fruit juice.

Be sparing with the seasoning and adjust before serving.

Thickening agents. Casseroles and stews may be thickened before slow cooking. Follow the method in the recipes. Some gravies are thickened after cooking. Flour or cornflour is mixed with a little cold water or stock then added to the Slo-Cooker during the final 30 minutes of cooking. Alternatively, gravy or sauce may be thickened in a separate pan just before serving.

Add cream, milk, and egg yolks during the final 30 minutes of cooking.

If you have a Slo-Cooker with a removable pot, pastry and scone toppings can be added and finished off in the oven for final cooking.

When adapting recipes for slow cooking consult similar ones within this section for guidance on cooking times.

Cooking times for joints vary according to size, shape, quality, the proportions of meat, fat and bone and personal tastes. Use the following times for guidance. . . .

Cook joints for 30 minutes on High setting then switch to Low for: 4–6 hours (3–5 hours High for pork) if 2–3½ lb. (1–1.6 kg.); 5–7 hours (4–6 hours High for pork) if 3½–5 lb. (1.6–2.3 kg.).

Beef Goulash

 Serves 6

INGREDIENTS

	Imperial	Metric	American
Stewing steak, cut into cubes	2½ lb.	1 kg.	2½ lb.
Seasoned flour	3–4 tbsp.	3–4 tbsp.	3–4 tbsp.
Cooking oil	3 tbsp.	3 tbsp.	3 tbsp.
Onions, chopped	3	3	3
Green peppers, de-seeded and sliced	2	2	2
Beef stock	½ pt.	300 ml.	1¼ cups
Canned tomatoes	14 oz.	397 g.	1 lb.
Tomato purée or paste	3 tbsp.	3 tbsp.	3 tbsp.
Paprika pepper	3 tsp.	3 tsp.	3 tsp.
Bouquet garni	1	1	1
For garnish :			
Sour cream or natural, unsweetened yoghurt			

Pre-heat Slo-Cooker on High for 20 minutes. Coat the meat with seasoned flour. Heat the cooking oil in a large pan and brown the meat lightly. Stir in the onions and peppers and cook for a further 2–3 minutes. Add the remaining ingredients, except cream, bring to the boil and transfer to Slo-Cooker. Cook on High for 30 minutes then switch to Low for 6–10 hours. Before serving, remove bouquet garni, adjust seasoning if necessary and stir the Goulash well.

Add a swirl of soured cream or yoghurt. This dish is superb served simply with dressed salad.

COOKING TIME
Pre-heat 20 minutes
High 30 minutes
Low 6–10 hours

Boiled Beef with Dumplings

 Serves 6

INGREDIENTS

	Imperial	Metric	American
Cooking oil	2 tbsp.	30 ml.	2 tbsp.
Beef joint, such as silverside or brisket	3 lb.	1½ kg.	3 lb.
Salt and pepper			
Onions, sliced	2	2	2
Carrots, sliced	4	4	4
Water	1 pt.	500 ml.	2½ cups
Dumplings :			
Self-raising flour or flour sifted with 1 tsp. baking powder	4 oz.	100 g.	1 cup
Shredded or finely chopped suet	2 oz.	50 g.	generous ¼ cup
Salt and pepper			
Water to mix			

Pre-heat Slo-Cooker on High for 20 minutes. Heat the cooking oil in a large pan and brown the seasoned joint on all sides. Transfer to Slo-Cooker. In the same oil sauté the onions and carrots gently for 3–4 minutes. Add the water, bring to the boil then pour the mixture around the beef in Slo-Cooker. Cook on High for 30 minutes then switch to Low for 6–9 hours. For rare beef add the dumplings after 5 hours.

Switch to High and prepare the dumplings. Mix the flour, suet and seasoning into a firm dough with water. Divide into eight balls and drop them into the juice around the beef. Cook on High for 30 minutes.

COOKING TIME
Pre-heat 20 minutes
High 30 minutes
Low 6–9 hours

Crown Roast of Lamb

 Serves 6

INGREDIENTS

	Imperial	Metric	American
Best end neck of Lamb	2 pcs. (12 ribs)	2 pcs. (12 ribs)	2 pcs. (12 ribs)
Salt and pepper			
Stuffing:			
Stale breadcrumbs	6 oz	175 g.	3 cups
Celery, finely chopped	4 oz.	100 g.	$\frac{1}{4}$ lb.
Onion, finely chopped	4 oz.	100 g.	$\frac{1}{4}$ lb.
Salt	2 tsp.	2 tsp.	2 tsp.
Pepper	$\frac{1}{2}$ tsp.	$\frac{1}{2}$ tsp.	$\frac{1}{2}$ tsp.
Dried sage	2 tsp.	2 tsp.	2 tsp.
Butter, melted	1 oz.	25 g.	2 tbsp.
Water			

Pre-heat Slo-Cooker on High for 20 minutes. Using a sharp knife trim the meat from the tip of each rib leaving about 1½ inches (4 cm.) exposed. Place the two ends of each joint together—bones outside—and fasten with string to form a crown. Season the inside with salt and pepper. Mix together the ingredients for the stuffing, binding with a little water if necessary.

Press the stuffing firmly into the centre of the crown. Heat the cooking oil in a frying pan and brown the outside of the joint. Place the meat in the Slo-Cooker so that it sits evenly. Cook on High for 30 minutes then switch to Low for 7–9 hours.

Lift the joint carefully onto a serving dish and keep warm. Switch the Slo-Cooker to High and thicken the remaining juices with some cornflour mixed with a little cold water or stock (about 30 minutes). Just before serving, remove the string from the joint and place a cutlet frill on the tip of each bone.

COOKING TIME
Pre-heat 20 minutes
High 30 minutes
Low 7–9 hours

CHECKPOINT
Ask the butcher to chop between the joints at the thick end of each cutlet so that the joint will curve. To enable easy removal of the cooked joint from the Slo-Cooker form a double strip of foil long enough to go down each side and across the bottom of the Slo-Cooker. Sit the joint on top.

Beef in the Pot

 Serves 8

INGREDIENTS

	Imperial	Metric	American
Cooking oil	2 tbsp.	30 ml.	2 tbsp.
Beef joint, such as back rib	4 lb.	1.8 kg.	4 lb.
Salt and pepper			
Onion, sliced	1 large	1 large	1 large
Carrots, sliced	2	2	2
Beef stock	½ pt.	300 ml.	1¼ cups
French mustard	3 tsp.	3 tsp.	3 tsp.
Worcestershire sauce	1 tbsp.	15 ml.	1 tbsp.
Bay leaves	2	2	2

Pre-heat Slo-Cooker on High for 20 minutes. Heat the cooking oil in a large pan and brown the seasoned joint on all sides. Transfer to Slo-Cooker. In the same oil sauté the onion and carrots gently for 2–3 minutes. Add the remaining ingredients, bring to the boil and pour round the beef in the Slo-Cooker. Cook on High for 30 minutes then switch to Low for 7–10 hours. Lift the beef onto a serving dish and keep warm. Strain the juices from the Slo-Cooker. In a small pan mix some flour or cornflour with a little water to form a smooth paste. Stir in the beef juices and bring to the boil. Serve immediately.

COOKING TIME
Pre-heat 20 minutes
High 30 minutes
Low 7–10 hours

TO FREEZE
Leftover slices should be arranged on a foil tray with gravy poured over. Cover and freeze. Defrost and re-heat in the foil tray.

Beefburgers in Tomato Sauce

 Serves 4

INGREDIENTS

	Imperial	Metric	American
Minced beef	1 lb.	450 g.	1 lb.
Breadcrumbs, fresh	4 oz.	100 g.	2 cups
Onion, minced	1 small	1 small	1 small
Mixed herbs	2 tsp.	2 tsp.	2 tsp.
Salt and pepper			
Butter	1 oz.	25 g.	2 tbsp.
Canned condensed Cream of Tomato soup	10½ oz.	298 g.	medium can
Beef stock cube	1	1	1
Water	¼ pt.	150 ml.	⅔ cup

Pre-heat Slo-Cooker on High for 20 minutes. Mix together the minced beef, breadcrumbs, onion, herbs and seasoning. Shape into eight beefburgers. Heat the butter in a frying pan and brown the beefburgers quickly on both sides. Transfer to Slo-Cooker. Carefully mix together the tomato soup and beef stock cube (dissolved in the water). Add this mixture to the remaining butter and juices in the frying pan and bring to the boil. Pour the sauce over the beefburgers in the Slo-Cooker. Cook on High for 30 minutes then switch to Low for 3–4 hours.

COOKING TIME
Pre-heat 20 minutes
High 30 minutes
Low 3–4 hours

TO FREEZE
Arrange the beefburgers on a foil tray and pour the sauce over. Cover and freeze.

Beef Stroganoff

  Serves 4

INGREDIENTS

	Imperial	Metric	American
Butter	2 oz.	50 g.	$\frac{1}{4}$ cup
Onions, chopped	2	2	2
Braising steak, cut into strips across the grain	$1\frac{1}{2}$ lb.	700 g.	$1\frac{1}{2}$ lb.
Seasoned flour	2 tbsp.	2 tbsp.	2 tbsp.
Beef stock	$\frac{1}{2}$ pt.	300 ml.	$1\frac{1}{4}$ cups
Mushrooms, sliced	4 oz.	100 g.	$\frac{1}{4}$ lb.
Mixed herbs	1 tsp.	1 tsp.	1 tsp.
Tomato purée or paste	1 tbsp.	1 tbsp.	1 tbsp.
French mustard	2 tsp.	2 tsp.	2 tsp.
Single or thin cream	$\frac{1}{4}$ pt.	150 ml.	$\frac{2}{3}$ cup
Chopped parsley	1 tbsp.	1 tbsp.	1 tbsp.

Pre-heat Slo-Cooker on High for 20 minutes. Heat the butter in a large pan and gently sauté the onions until they begin to turn transparent. Toss the braising steak in the seasoned flour and add to the onions. Stir the mixture over the heat until the meat is lightly browned. Stir in the remaining ingredients and bring to the boil. Transfer to Slo-Cooker. Cook on High for 30 minutes then switch to Low for 6–10 hours. Just before serving, stir well, swirl the cream on top of the Stroganoff and garnish with chopped parsley.

COOKING TIME
Pre-heat 20 minutes
High 30 minutes
Low 6–10 hours

TO FREEZE
Omit cream and parsley. Pack into rigid polythene or foil container, cover and freeze. Stir in the cream after reheating, but do not boil. Garnish with chopped parsley.

Beef in Red Wine

 Serves 6

INGREDIENTS

	Imperial	Metric	American
Cooking oil	1 tbsp.	15 ml.	1 tbsp.
Butter	1 oz.	25 g.	2 tbsp.
Streaky bacon, chopped	8 oz.	225 g.	$\frac{1}{2}$ lb.
Cloves garlic, crushed	2	2	2
Stewing steak, cut into cubes	$2\frac{1}{2}$ lb.	1 kg.	$2\frac{1}{2}$ lb.
Flour	4 tbsp.	4 tbsp.	4 tbsp.
Red wine	$\frac{1}{2}$ pt.	300 ml.	$1\frac{1}{4}$ cups
Bay leaves	2	2	2
Whole small onions, skinned	12	12	12
Salt			
Black pepper			

Pre-heat Slo-Cooker on High for 20 minutes. Heat the cooking oil and butter in a large pan and sauté the bacon and garlic gently for 2–3 minutes. Add the steak and stir over the heat until lightly browned. Stir in the flour then slowly add the red wine, followed by bay leaves, onions and seasoning to taste. Bring to the boil and transfer to Slo-Cooker.

Cook on High for 30 minutes then switch to Low for 6–10 hours. Remove bay leaves. Stir before serving and adjust seasoning if necessary.

COOKING TIME
Pre-heat 20 minutes
High 30 minutes
Low 6–10 hours

TO FREEZE
Omit garlic. Pack into rigid polythene or foil container, cover and freeze. Add garlic or garlic salt at reheating stage.

Braised Oxtail

 Serves 4

INGREDIENTS	Imperial	Metric	American
Cooking oil	2 tbsp.	30 ml.	2 tbsp.
Streaky bacon	4 oz.	100 g.	$\frac{1}{4}$ lb.
Onion, finely sliced	1 large	1 large	1 large
Carrots, thinly sliced	8 oz.	225 g.	$\frac{1}{2}$ lb.
Oxtail joints	2 lb.	900 g.	2 lb.
Seasoned flour			
Beef stock	1 pt.	600 ml.	$2\frac{1}{2}$ cups
Bouquet garni			
Redcurrant jelly (optional)	1 tbsp.	1 tbsp.	1 tbsp.

Pre-heat Slo-Cooker on High for 30 minutes. Heat the cooking oil in a large pan and sauté the bacon, onion and carrots gently for 3–4 minutes. Transfer to Slo-Cooker. Coat the oxtail joints with seasoned flour and, using the same pan, brown them on all sides. Stir in the beef stock and add the bouquet garni. Bring to the boil then transfer to Slo-Cooker. Stir well. Cook on High for 30 minutes, then switch to Low for 8–10 hours. Just before serving, stir well, remove bouquet garni and add the redcurrant jelly (optional).

COOKING TIME
Pre-heat 20 minutes
High 30 minutes
Low 8–10 hours

TO FREEZE
Pack into rigid polythene or foil container, cover and freeze.

Honeyed Lamb

 Serves 8

INGREDIENTS

	Imperial	Metric	American
Butter	1½ oz.	40 g.	3 tbsp.
Leg lamb	4½ lb.	2 kg.	4½ lb.
Salt and pepper			
Cornflour or cornstarch	3 tbsp.	3 tbsp.	3 tbsp.
Good pinch ginger			
Cider	½ pt.	300 ml.	1¼ cups
Clear honey	4 tbsp	4 tbsp.	4 tbsp.
Dried rosemary	1 tbsp.	1 tbsp.	1 tbsp.

Pre-heat Slo-Cooker on High for 20 minutes. Heat the butter in a large pan and brown the lamb on all sides, seasoning with salt and pepper. Transfer the lamb to the Slo-Cooker. Stir the cornflour and ginger into the remaining butter and then add the cider gradually, stirring all the time. Bring to the boil. Stir in the honey and when melted, pour the sauce over the lamb, coating it well. Sprinkle over the rosemary. Cook on High for 30 minutes then switch to Low for 6–10 hours. If possible, baste the joint once or twice during this period. Place the joint on a carving dish and serve the sauce separately.

COOKING TIME
Pre-heat 20 minutes
High 30 minutes
Low 6–10 hours

TO FREEZE
Leftover slices of lamb may be frozen in a foil tray with some of the sauce poured over.

CHECKPOINT
When buying a leg of lamb for Slo-Cooking, you may need to ask your butcher to cut the bone near the end of the leg so that it fits neatly into the Slo-Cooker.

Sweet and Sour Pork Chops

 Serves 4

INGREDIENTS

	Imperial	Metric	American
Pork chops	4	4	4
Seasoned flour			
Butter	2 oz.	50 g.	$\frac{1}{4}$ cup
Onions, finely chopped	2	2	2
Soy sauce	4 tbsp.	60 ml.	4 tbsp.
Tomato purée or paste	4 tbsp.	4 tbsp.	4 tbsp.
Soft brown sugar	4 tbsp.	4 tbsp.	4 tbsp.
Sherry	$\frac{1}{4}$ pt.	150 ml.	$\frac{2}{3}$ cup

Pre-heat Slo-Cooker on high for 30 minutes. Trim excess fat from pork chops and coat with seasoned flour. Heat the butter in a large pan and quickly brown the chops on all sides. Transfer to Slo-Cooker. In the same butter sauté the onions gently till transparent. Stir in the remaining ingredients and bring to the boil. Pour over the pork chops in the Slo-Cooker. Cook on High for 30 minutes then switch to Low for 4–5 hours.

COOKING TIME
Pre-heat 20 minutes
High 30 minutes
Low 4–5 hours

Pork in Cider

  Serves 4

INGREDIENTS

	Imperial	Metric	American
Cooking oil	1 tbsp.	15 ml.	1 tbsp.
Butter	1 oz.	25 g.	2 tbsp.
Onion, sliced	1	1	1
Sticks or stalks celery, sliced	2	2	2
Cooking apple, peeled, cored and chopped	1 large	1 large	1 large
Lean pork such as shoulder, cut in cubes	$1\frac{3}{4}$ lb.	800 g.	$1\frac{3}{4}$ lb.
Flour	2 tbsp.	2 tbsp.	2 tbsp.
Dry cider	$\frac{1}{2}$ pt.	300 ml.	$1\frac{1}{4}$ cups
Salt and pepper			
Bouquet garni			

Pre-heat Slo-Cooker on High for 20 minutes. Heat the cooking oil and butter in a large pan and sauté the onion, celery and apple gently for 2–3 minutes. Transfer to Slo-Cooker. In the same pan brown the pork lightly. Mix the flour with a little dry cider then stir in the rest. Add this to the pork along with salt and black pepper and bouquet garni. Bring to the boil, stirring well. Transfer to Slo-Cooker and stir the mixture. Cook on High for 30 minutes then switch to Low for 6–10 hours. Remove bouquet garni before serving.

COOKING TIME
Pre-heat 20 minutes
High 30 minutes
Low 6–10 hours

TO FREEZE
Pack into rigid polythene or foil container, cover and freeze.

Lamb Cutlets in Red Wine Sauce

 Serves 4

INGREDIENTS

	Imperial	Metric	American
Cooking oil	2 tbsp.	30 ml.	2 tbsp.
Onions, cut into fine rings	2	2	2
Salt and pepper			
Lamb cutlets	8	8	8
Cornflour or cornstarch	1 tbsp.	1 tbsp.	1 tbsp.
Red wine	$\frac{1}{2}$ pt.	300 ml.	$1\frac{1}{4}$ cups
Dried rosemary	2 tsp.	2 tsp.	2 tsp.

Pre-heat Slo-Cooker on High for 20 minutes. Heat the cooking oil in a large pan and sauté the onions gently till beginning to turn transparent. Transfer to Slo-Cooker. Season the lamb cutlets with salt and pepper and brown all sides quickly in the same pan. Arrange on top of the onions in the Slo-Cooker. Mix the cornflour into the remaining fat in the pan, then slowly add the red wine, stirring well. Add the rosemary. Bring to the boil, pour the sauce over the cutlets in the Slo-Cooker. Cook on High for 30 minutes then switch to Low for 3–4 hours.

COOKING TIME
Pre-heat 20 minutes
High 30 minutes
Low 3–4 hours

Braised Danish Bacon

  Serves 6

INGREDIENTS

	Imperial	Metric	American
Danish bacon joint, such as prime collar or gammon	2 lb.	1 kg.	2 lb.
Brown sugar	1 tbsp.	1 tbsp.	1 tbsp.
Tomatoes, skinned and coarsely chopped	8 oz.	225 g.	$\frac{1}{2}$ lb.
Onions, finely sliced	8 oz.	225 g.	$\frac{1}{2}$ lb.
Black pepper	2 tbsp.	2 tbsp.	2 tbsp.
Water	2 tbsp.	2 tbsp.	2 tbsp.
Mushrooms, sliced	4 oz.	100 g.	$\frac{1}{4}$ lb.
Lemon juice	2 tbsp.	30 ml.	2 tbsp.
Chopped parsley			

Pre-heat Slo-Cooker on High for 20 minutes. Place the bacon joint in a large pan and cover with cold water. Bring slowly to the boil and pour the water away. Cut off the rind and snip into the fat at intervals. Sprinkle the joint with the brown sugar and place under a pre-heated grill to melt and brown. (If your Slo-Cooker has a removable pot this can be done in the earthenware pot.) Arrange the tomatoes and onions in layers in the Slo-Cooker. Season with black pepper and add the water. Place the browned bacon joint on top. Cook on High for 30 minutes then switch to Low for 6–9 hours.

In a separate pan cook the mushrooms in a little water with the lemon juice for about 3 minutes. Drain and use to garnish the dish. Sprinkle chopped parsley over.

COOKING TIME
Pre-heat 20 minutes
High 30 minutes
Low 6–9 hours

Beef Olives

 Serves 4

INGREDIENTS

	Imperial	Metric	American
Braising steak	1 lb.	450 g.	1 lb.
Stuffing :			
Fresh breadcrumbs	2 oz.	50 g.	1 cup
Shredded or finely chopped suet	1 oz.	25 g.	2 tbsp.
Mixed herbs	½ tsp.	½ tsp.	½ tsp.
Chopped parsley	1 tsp.	1 tsp.	1 tsp.
Salt and pepper			
Egg, beaten	1	1	1
Lemon juice	1 tsp.	1 tsp.	1 tsp.
Cooking oil	2 tbsp.	2 tbsp.	2 tbsp.
Onion, sliced	1	1	1
Flour	1 oz.	25 g.	¼ cup
Beef stock	¾ pt.	400 ml.	2 cups
Salt and pepper			

Pre-heat Slo-Cooker on High for 20 minutes. Cut the steak into about 8 thin slices across the grain—about 4 inches (10 cm) square. Mix together the stuffing ingredients and spread a little onto each slice. Roll up and secure each with cotton. Heat the cooking oil in a large pan and lightly brown the meat rolls. Remove. In the same pan sauté the onion gently until beginning to turn transparent.

Add the flour and cook until brown. Gradually stir in the stock and season to taste. Bring to the boil, stirring well. Transfer to Slo-Cooker and arrange the meat on top. Cook on High for 30 minutes then switch to Low for 5–9 hours. Remove the cotton from the meat and arrange on a serving dish. Keep warm. Strain the gravy and reheat in a small pan if necessary. Pour over the meat just before serving.

COOKING TIME
Pre-heat 20 minutes
High 30 minutes
Low 5–9 hours

TO FREEZE
Arrange the meat on a foil tray and pour gravy round. Cover and freeze. Defrost in room temperature and re-heat in foil tray.

CHECKPOINT
For this dish you will need to buy a piece of lean braising steak of a shape suitable to be cut into 4 inch (10 cm.) squares. Use a sharp knife.

Beef in Beer

 Serves 6

INGREDIENTS	Imperial	Metric	American
Cooking oil	2 tbsp.	30 ml.	2 tbsp.
Onions, chopped	1 lb.	450 g.	1 lb.
Bacon, chopped	4 oz.	100 g.	$\frac{1}{4}$ lb.
Stewing steak, cut into cubes	$2\frac{1}{2}$ lb.	1 kg.	$2\frac{1}{2}$ lb.
Seasoned flour	3 tbsp.	3 tbsp.	3 tbsp.
Brown ale	$\frac{3}{4}$ pt.	400 ml.	2 cups
French mustard	2 tsp.	2 tsp.	2 tsp.
Sugar	3 tsp.	3 tsp.	3 tsp.
Mixed herbs	$\frac{1}{2}$ tsp.	$\frac{1}{2}$ tsp.	$\frac{1}{2}$ tsp.

Topping: 6 slices French bread and French Mustard

Pre-heat Slo-Cooker on High for 20 minutes. Heat cooking oil in large pan and sauté the onions and bacon gently until transparent. Transfer to Slo-Cooker. Toss the steak in the seasoned flour and brown lightly in the same oil. Add brown ale slowly, stirring all the time. Add mustard, sugar and herbs. Bring to the boil and transfer to Slo-Cooker. Stir well, cook on High for 30 minutes then switch to Low for 6–10 hours.

To prepare topping: If your Slo-Cooker has a removable pot arrange slices of the bread spread with French mustard—mustard side down—on the meat and brown under a pre-heated grill. If your Slo-Cooker has a fixed pot, toast one side of the bread first, spread the other with French Mustard and arrange mustard side down on the meat to serve.

COOKING TIME
Pre-heat 20 minutes
High 30 minutes
Low 6–10 hours

TO FREEZE
Omit topping. Pack into rigid polythene or foil container, cover and freeze. Prepare topping just before serving.

Lamb in Mushroom Sauce

 Serves 4–6

INGREDIENTS

	Imperial	Metric	American
Cooking oil	1 tbsp.	15 ml.	1 tbsp.
Butter	1 oz.	25 g.	2 tbsp.
Onions, thinly sliced	2	2	2
Clove garlic, crushed	1	1	1
Green pepper, de-seeded and sliced	1	1	1
Lean lamb such as leg, cut into cubes	$1\frac{3}{4}$ lb.	800 g.	$1\frac{3}{4}$ lb.
Dried marjoram	1 tsp.	1 tsp.	1 tsp.
Salt and pepper			
Canned condensed mushroom soup	$10\frac{1}{2}$ oz.	298 g.	medium can
Water	$\frac{1}{4}$ pt.	150 ml.	$\frac{2}{3}$ cup
Mushrooms, sliced	4 oz.	100 g.	$\frac{1}{4}$ lb.

Pre-heat Slo-Cooker on High for 20 minutes. Heat the oil and butter in a large pan and sauté the onions, garlic and green pepper gently for 2–3 minutes. Stir in the lamb and cook for a further 2–3 minutes. Add the marjoram and seasoning, then the soup (mixed well with the water) and mushrooms. Bring to the boil slowly and transfer to Slo-Cooker.

Cook on High for 30 minutes, then switch to Low for 5–9 hours.

COOKING TIME
Pre-heat 20 minutes
High 30 minutes
Low 5–9 hours

TO FREEZE
Omit garlic. Pack into rigid polythene or foil container, cover and freeze. Add garlic at re-heating stage or season with garlic salt.

Navarin of Lamb

 Serves 6–8

INGREDIENTS

	Imperial	Metric	American
Best end neck lamb chops	$2\frac{1}{2}$ lb.	1 kg.	$2\frac{1}{2}$ lb.
Salt and pepper			
Butter	$\frac{1}{2}$ oz.	15 g.	1 tbsp.
Carrots, sliced	3 large	3 large	3 large
Onions, chopped	2	2	2
Potatoes, cut in $\frac{1}{2}$ in. (1 cm.) cubes	1 lb.	450 g.	1 lb.
Flour	2–3 tbsp.	2–3 tbsp.	2–3 tbsp.
Beef stock	1 pt.	500 ml.	$2\frac{1}{2}$ cups
Sugar	2 tsp.	2 tsp.	2 tsp.
Tomato purée or paste	3 tbsp.	3 tbsp.	3 tbsp.
Bouquet garni			

Pre-heat Slo-Cooker on High for 20 minutes. Season the lamb chops with salt and pepper. Heat the butter in a large pan and brown the chops quickly on all sides. Transfer to Slo-Cooker. In the same pan, sauté the vegetables gently for 3–4 minutes. Mix the flour first with a little beef stock, then the remainder. Add this and the remaining ingredients to the vegetables. Bring to the boil, stirring continuously. Transfer to Slo-Cooker and stir well. Cook on High for 30 minutes then switch to Low for 7–9 hours.

Remove bouquet garni before serving and adjust seasoning if necessary.

COOKING TIME
Pre-heat 20 minutes
High 30 minutes
Low 7–9 hours

Spanish Pork

 Serves 6–8

INGREDIENTS

	Imperial	Metric	American
Lean pork, cut into cubes	1½ lb.	700 g.	1½ lb.
Seasoned flour	2 tbsp.	2 tbsp.	2 tbsp.
Butter	2 oz.	50 g.	¼ cup
Onion, chopped	1 large	1 large	1 large
Green peppers, de-seeded and chopped	2	2	2
Canned tomatoes	1¾ lb.	794 g.	large can
Chilli sauce	1–2 tsp.	1–2 tsp.	1–2 tsp.
Sugar	2 tsp.	2 tsp.	2 tsp.
Salt and pepper			

Pre-heat Slo-Cooker on High for 20 minutes. Toss the pork in the seasoned flour. Heat the butter in a large pan and lightly brown the pork cubes. Stir in the onion and peppers and cook gently for a further 2–3 minutes. Add the remaining ingredients and bring to the boil, stirring continuously. Transfer to Slo-Cooker. Cook on High for 30 minutes then switch to Low for 7–10 hours. Adjust seasoning if necessary. Delicious served with green salad.

COOKING TIME
Pre-heat 20 minutes
High 30 minutes
Low 7–10 hours

TO FREEZE
Pack into rigid polythene or foil container, cover and freeze.

Piquant Bacon

  Serves 6

INGREDIENTS

	Imperial	Metric	American
Unsmoked bacon, cut into cubes	2½ lb.	1 kg.	2½ lb.
Butter	2 oz.	50 g.	¼ cup
Onion, chopped	1 large	1 large	1 large
Carrots, sliced	2	2	2
Flour	2 tbsp.	2 tbsp.	2 tbsp.
Chicken stock or white wine	½ pt.	300 ml.	1¼ cups
Vinegar	3 tbsp.	3 tbsp.	3 tbsp.
Black pepper	½ tsp.	½ tsp.	½ tsp.
Ground cloves	pinch	pinch	pinch

Pre-heat Slo-Cooker on High for 20 minutes. Place the bacon cubes in a large pan and cover with cold water. Bring slowly to the boil. Discard the water and dry the bacon on kitchen paper. Heat the butter in a large pan and brown the bacon lightly. Transfer to Slo-Cooker. In the same butter sauté the onion and carrots for 2–3 minutes. Stir in the flour then gradually add the chicken stock/wine and vinegar. Bring to the boil and add the pepper and cloves. Transfer to Slo-Cooker and stir the mixture well. Cook on High for 30 minutes then switch to Low for 6–10 hours.

COOKING TIME
Pre-heat 20 minutes
High 30 minutes
Low 6–10 hours

TO FREEZE
Pack into rigid polythene or foil container, cover and freeze.

Kidney Ragout

  Serves 4

INGREDIENTS	Imperial	Metric	American
Lambs' kidneys, skinned, halved, cores removed	*8–10*	*8–10*	*8–10*
Salt and pepper			
Butter	*1 oz.*	*25 g.*	*2 tbsp.*
Onions, chopped	*2*	*2*	*2*
Flour	*3 tbsp.*	*3 tbsp.*	*3 tbsp.*
Beef stock	*½ pt.*	*300 ml.*	*1¼ cups*
Tomato purée or paste	*2 tbsp.*	*2 tbsp.*	*2 tbsp.*
Mushrooms, sliced	*4 oz.*	*100 g.*	*¼ lb.*

Pre-heat Slo-Cooker on High for 20 minutes. Season the kidneys with salt and pepper. Heat the butter in a large pan and sauté the kidneys and the onion gently for 2–3 minutes. Stir in the flour then gradually add the beef stock and tomato purée. Bring to the boil, add the mushrooms and transfer to Slo-Cooker. Cook on High for 30 minutes then switch to Low for 5–8 hours. Adjust seasoning if necessary. Serve on a bed of rice or creamed potato.

COOKING TIME
Pre-heat 20 minutes
High 30 minutes
Low 5–8 hours

TO FREEZE
Pack into rigid polythene or foil container, cover and freeze.

Pork and Pineapple Curry

 Serves 6

INGREDIENTS

	Imperial	Metric	American
Flour	1½ oz.	40 g.	⅓ cup
Salt	1 tsp.	1 tsp.	1 tsp.
Lean pork, cut into cubes	2 lb.	1 kg.	2 lb.
Cooking oil	2 tbsp.	2 tbsp.	2 tbsp
Onion, finely chopped	1 large	1 large	1 large
Curry powder	1 tbsp.	1 tbsp.	1 tbsp.
Paprika pepper	1 tbsp.	1 tbsp.	1 tbsp.
Chicken stock	½ pt.	300 ml.	1¼ cups
Dried red chillies	2	2	2
Mango chutney	1 tbsp.	1 tbsp.	1 tbsp.
Worcestershire sauce	1 tsp.	1 tsp.	1 tsp.
Canned pineapple cubes, including syrup	1 lb.	450 g.	1 lb.
Bay leaves	2	2	2

Pre-heat Slo-Cooker on high for 20 minutes.

Mix together the flour and salt then toss the pork pieces till coated. Heat the cooking oil in a large pan and brown the meat gently on all sides. Transfer to Slo-Cooker. In the same oil sauté the onion until soft. Add the remaining ingredients, bring to the boil and transfer to Slo-Cooker. Stir the curry well. Cook on High for 30 minutes then switch to Low for 5–7 hours. Remove bay leaves and stir well before serving with boiled rice.

COOKING TIME
Pre-heat 20 minutes
High 30 minutes
Low 5–7 hours

TO FREEZE
Omit pineapple. Pack into rigid polythene or foil container, cover and freeze. Add pineapple at reheating stage.

Note: Try this curry with lamb to replace the pork for a change.

Norfolk Pork

  Serves 8

INGREDIENTS	Imperial	Metric	American
Pork joint, such as hand extending to knuckle	4½ lb.	2 kg.	4½ lb.
Seasoned flour	2 tbsp.	2 tbsp.	2 tbsp.
Dry mustard	1 tsp.	1 tsp.	1 tsp.
Butter	1 oz.	25 g.	2 tbsp.
Onion, finely chopped	1	1	1
Eating apple, peeled, cored and chopped	1	1	1
Onion stock cube, crumbled	1	1	1
Water	½ pt.	300 ml.	1¼ cups

Pre-Heat Slo-Cooker on High for 20 minutes. Cut the rind off the pork joint. Mix together the seasoned flour and dry mustard and use to coat the pork joint thoroughly. Heat the butter in a large pan and brown the joint on all sides. Transfer to Slo-Cooker. In the same pan sauté the onion gently until transparent. Stir in the remaining ingredients, bring to the boil and pour round the pork in the Slo-Cooker. Cook on High for 4½–6 hours.

Lift the joint out of the Slo-Cooker and place on a serving dish. Strain the remaining juices into a small pan and thicken if necessary with some cornflour mixed with a little cold water. Bring to the boil and adjust seasoning. Serve separately.

COOKING TIME
Pre-heat 20 minutes
High 4½–6 hours

TO FREEZE
Leftover slices of pork should be arranged on a foil tray with sauce poured over. Cover and freeze. Defrost and re-heat in the foil tray.

Mustard Braised Tongues

 Serves 4

INGREDIENTS	Imperial	Metric	American
Lambs' tongues	8	8	8
Butter	1 oz.	25 g.	2 tbsp.
Onion, finely chopped	2	2	2
Carrots, chopped	2	2	2
Flour	2 tbsp.	2 tbsp.	2 tbsp.
Beef stock	½ pt.	300 ml.	1¼ cups
Wine vinegar	1 tbsp.	1 tbsp.	1 tbsp.
Dry mustard	3 tsp.	3 tsp.	3 tsp.
Salt and pepper			

Pre-heat Slo-Cooker on High for 20 minutes. Wash and trim the tongues and arrange in the Slo-Cooker. In a frying pan, heat the butter and sauté the onions and carrots gently for 3–4 minutes. Stir in the flour then gradually add the beef stock and wine vinegar. Bring to the boil and add the mustard. Season to taste. Transfer to Slo-Cooker. Cook on High for 30 minutes then switch to Low for 6–10 hours. Before serving adjust seasoning if necessary.

COOKING TIME
Pre-heat 20 minutes
High 30 minutes

Liver Casserole

 Serves 6

INGREDIENTS	Imperial	Metric	American
Butter	1½ oz.	40 g.	3 tbsp.
Onions, chopped	2	2	2
Rashers or slices bacon, chopped	4	4	4
Lambs' liver, cut into strips ½ in. (1 cm.) wide	1½ lb.	700 g.	1½ lb.
Seasoned flour			
Canned tomatoes	14 oz.	397 g.	medium can
Beef stock	¼–½ pt.	150–300 ml.	⅔–1¼ cups
Worcestershire sauce	1 tbsp.	15 ml.	1 tbsp.

Pre-heat Slo-Cooker on High for 20 minutes. Heat the butter in a large pan and sauté the onions and bacon gently until transparent. Toss the liver strips in the seasoned flour, add to the onions and continue cooking for 2–3 minutes, stirring well. Add the remaining ingredients, bring to the boil and transfer to Slo-Cooker. Cook on High for 30 minutes then switch to Low for 3–5 hours.

COOKING TIME
Pre-heat 20 minutes
High 30 minutes
Low 3–5 hours

Sausage Supper

 Serves 6

INGREDIENTS	Imperial	Metric	American
Cooking oil	2 tbsp.	30 ml.	2 tbsp.
Onion, chopped	1	1	1
Potatoes, thinly sliced	1 lb.	450 g.	1 lb.
Salt and black pepper			
Skinless beef sausages, cut in half	1 lb.	450 g.	1 lb.
Canned baked beans	15¾ oz.	447 g.	medium can
Mushrooms, halved	4 oz.	100 g.	¼ lb.
Chilli powder	2 tsp.	2 tsp.	2 tsp.
Tomato purée or paste	1 tbsp.	1 tbsp.	1 tbsp.
Water	¼ pt.	150 ml.	⅔ cup

Pre-heat Slo-Cooker on High for 20 minutes. Heat the cooking oil in a large pan and sauté the onion and potatoes gently for 4–5 minutes. Season with salt and black pepper. Add the remaining ingredients and bring to the boil. Transfer to Slo-Cooker. Cook on High for 6–10 hours. Serve with warm crusty bread to make a filling meal.

COOKING TIME
Pre-heat 20 minutes
High 30 minutes
Low 6–10 hours

Savoury Pork Casserole

 Serves 4

INGREDIENTS	Imperial	Metric	American
Cooking oil	2 tbsp.	2 tbsp.	2 tbsp.
Pork tenderloin, cut into cubes	1½ lb.	700 g.	1½ lb.
Green pepper, deseeded and chopped	1	1	1
Large onions, thinly sliced	2	2	2
Mushrooms	8 oz.	225 g.	½ lb.
Flour	2 tbsp.	2 tbsp.	2 tbsp.
White wine	½ pt.	300 ml.	1¼ cups
Chicken stock	¼ pt.	150 ml.	⅔ cup
Tomato purée or paste	2 tbsp.	2 tbsp.	2 tbsp.
Salt			
Black pepper			
Dried sage	1 tsp.	1 tsp.	1 tsp.
Large tomatoes, skinned and sliced	4	4	4

Pre-heat Slo-Cooker on High for 20 minutes. Heat the cooking oil in a large pan and sauté the pork until lightly browned. Add the pepper, onions and mushrooms then stir in the flour. Add the wine, stock and tomato purée. Bring to the boil, stirring continuously. Season with salt and black pepper and add the sage and tomatoes. Transfer to Slo-Cooker. Cook on High for 30 minutes then switch to Low for 5–8 hours.

COOKING TIME
Pre-heat 20 minutes
High 30 minutes   Low 5–8 hours

TO FREEZE
Pack into rigid polythene or foil container, cover and freeze.

Braised Liver and Onions

 Serves 4

INGREDIENTS

	Imperial	Metric	American
Cooking oil	4 tbsp.	4 tbsp.	4 tbsp.
Large onions, sliced	2	2	2
Lamb's liver, thinly sliced	1 lb.	450 g.	1 lb.
Seasoned flour	2 oz.	50 g.	½ cup
Beef stock	¾ pt.	400 ml.	2 cups

Pre-heat Slo-Cooker on High for 20 minutes.
Heat half the cooking oil in a large pan and sauté the onions until golden. Transfer to Slo-Cooker. Coat the liver with seasoned flour. Add the remaining oil to the pan and cook the liver to seal it. Transfer to Slo-Cooker. Add the remaining flour to the pan and carefully stir in the stock. Bring to the boil, stirring all the time. Transfer to Slo-Cooker. Cook on High for 30 minutes then switch to Low for 3–5 hours. Serve with grilled bacon.

COOKING TIME
Pre-heat 20 minutes
High 30 minutes
Low 3–5 hours

Veal and Tomato Casserole

 Serves 4

INGREDIENTS

	Imperial	Metric	American
Cooking oil	2 tbsp.	30 ml.	2 tbsp.
Clove garlic, crushed	1	1	1
Lemon juice	2 tbsp.	30 ml.	2 tbsp.
Salt			
Freshly ground black pepper			
Thyme, dried	¼ tsp.	¼ tsp.	¼ tsp.
Stewing veal, cut into cubes	1½ lb.	700 g.	1½ lb.
Flour	2 tbsp.	2 tbsp.	2 tbsp.
Dry white wine	¼ pt.	150 ml.	⅔ cup
Canned tomatoes	14 oz.	397 g.	medium can

Mix together the cooking oil, garlic, lemon juice, salt, pepper and thyme, and use to coat the veal cubes. Leave the mixture to marinate for ½–1 hour, turning occasionally. Pre-heat Slo-Cooker on High for 20 minutes.
In a saucepan, mix the flour with the white wine to form a smooth paste. Stir in the tomatoes (including juice) and the veal mixture. Bring to the boil, stirring continuously. Transfer to Slo-Cooker. Cook on High for 30 minutes then switch to Low for 6–10 hours. Stir before serving and adjust seasoning if necessary.

COOKING TIME
Pre-heat 20 minutes
High 30 minutes
Low 6–10 hours

TO FREEZE
Pack into rigid polythene or foil container, cover and freeze.

Bacon Pot Roast with Sage

  Serves 8–10

INGREDIENTS

	Imperial	Metric	American
Unsmoked bacon joint such as collar	4½ lb.	2 kg.	4½ lb.
Cooking oil	1 tbsp.	15 ml.	1 tbsp.
Butter	1 oz.	25 g.	2 tbsp.
Onion, chopped	1 large	1 large	1 large
Eating apple, peeled, cored and chopped	1	1	1
Chopped fresh sage or dried sage	1 tbsp.	1 tbsp.	1 tbsp.
Water	1 tsp.	1 tsp.	1 tsp.
Black pepper			

Pre-heat Slo-Cooker on High for 20 minutes. Place the bacon joint in a large pan and cover with cold water. Bring to the boil slowly then discard the water. Dry joint with kitchen paper. Heat the cooking oil and butter in a large pan and brown the bacon on all sides. Transfer to Slo-Cooker. In the same pan sauté the onion until transparent. Add the remaining ingredients, bring to the boil and pour round the bacon in the Slo-Cooker. Cook on High for 30 minutes then switch to Low for 7–10 hours. Lift the bacon onto a serving dish and keep warm. Mix some flour with a little cold water to form a smooth paste. Add to the juices in the Slo-Cooker and switch to High for about 30 minutes. Alternatively thicken quickly in a saucepan. Adjust seasoning.

COOKING TIME
Pre-heat 20 minutes
High 30 minutes
Low 7–10 hours

TO FREEZE
Leftover slices of bacon may be placed in a foil tray with some sauce poured over. Cover and freeze. Defrost and reheat in the foil tray.

Steak and Kidney Pudding

 Serves 4

INGREDIENTS

	Imperial	Metric	American
Suet pastry :			
Self raising flour, or flour sifted with 2 tsp. baking powder	*8 oz.*	*225 g.*	*2 cups*
Salt	*pinch*	*pinch*	*pinch*
Shredded or finely chopped suet	*4 oz.*	*100 g.*	*¾ cup*
Water	*¼ pt.*	*150 ml.*	*⅔ cup*
Filling :			
Stewing steak, cut into cubes	*12 oz.*	*350 g.*	*¾ lb.*
Sheep kidneys, skinned and chopped	*4 oz.*	*100 g.*	*¼ lb.*
Seasoned flour			
Onion, finely chopped	*1*	*1*	*1*
Salt and pepper			
Beef stock	*¼ pt.*	*150 ml.*	*⅔ cup*

Pre-heat Slo-Cooker on High for 20 minutes. Sieve together the flour and salt and stir in the suet. Mix in the water to form an elastic dough. Roll two-thirds of the dough into a circle and use to line a greased 1½pt/1 litre basin. Roll the remaining dough into a circle to cover the pudding. Prepare the filling by coating the steak and kidney with seasoned flour. Mix in the onion and seasoning. Use the mixture to fill the pastry case.

Pour in the beef stock. Dampen the edges of the dough, cover with the remaining pastry and press the edges firmly together. Trim if necessary. Cover with foil or a double layer of greased greaseproof paper tied on with string. Make a pleat in this since the pudding will rise. Position the pudding in the Slo-Cooker and pour sufficient boiling water round to come half way up the sides. Cook on High for 5–8 hours.

COOKING TIME
Pre-heat 20 minutes
High 5–8 hours

Devon Bacon Casserole

 Serves 6

COOKING TIME
Pre-heat 20 minutes
High 30 minutes
Low 6–10 hours

INGREDIENTS

	Imperial	Metric	American
Unsmoked bacon, cut into cubes	2½ lb.	1 kg.	2½ lb.
Butter	1 oz.	25 g.	2 tbsp.
Flour	2 tbsp.	2 tbsp.	2 tbsp.
Dry cider	½ pt.	300 ml.	1¼ cups
Onion, chopped	2	2	2
Leeks, cut into rings	2	2	2
Tomatoes, skinned and sliced	6	6	6
Apple jelly	2 tbsp.	2 tbsp.	2 tbsp.
Bouquet garni	1	1	1
Black pepper			
Garnish:			
Butter	1½ oz.	40 g.	3 tbsp.
Eating apples, cored and cut into rings	2	2	2

TO FREEZE

Omit garnish. Pack into rigid polythene or foil container, cover and freeze. Prepare garnish at re-heating stage.

Pre-heat Slo-Cooker on High for 20 minutes. Place the bacon cubes in a large pan and cover with cold water. Bring slowly to the boil, discard water, and dry the bacon well on kitchen paper. Heat the butter in a large pan and lightly brown the bacon. Stir in the flour and gradually add the cider. Add the remaining ingredients, except those for garnish, bring to the boil, then transfer to Slo-Cooker.

Cook on High for 30 minutes, then switch to Low for 6–10 hours. Stir before serving, remove bouquet garni and adjust seasoning if necessary.

To prepare the garnish, melt the butter in a pan and sauté the apple rings quickly, browning on both sides. Use these to decorate the top of the casserole.

Redcurrant Pork

  Serves 4

INGREDIENTS

	Imperial	Metric	American
Lean pork belly, cut into small pieces	*1½–2 lb.*	*¾–1 kg.*	*1½–2 lb.*
Onions, chopped	*2*	*2*	*2*
Carrots, thinly sliced	*2*	*2*	*2*
Flour	*2 tbsp.*	*2 tbsp.*	*2 tbsp.*
Chicken stock	*½ pt.*	*300 ml.*	*1¼ cups*
Redcurrant jelly	*3 tbsp.*	*3 tbsp.*	*3 tbsp.*
Salt and pepper			
Bay leaf	*1*	*1*	*1*
Stuffing :			
Stale breadcrumbs	*2 oz.*	*50 g.*	*1 cup*
Onion, finely chopped	*1*	*1*	*1*
Fresh sage leaves or dried sage	*5 ½ tsp.*	*5 ½ tsp.*	*5 ½ tsp.*
Salt	*1 tsp.*	*1 tsp.*	*1 tsp.*
Pepper	*¼ tsp.*	*¼ tsp.*	*¼ tsp.*
Egg, beaten	*1 small*	*1 small*	*1 small*
Milk			

Pre-heat Slo-Cooker on High for 20 minutes. Heat the pork pieces in a large pan until the fat begins to run out then brown them lightly on all sides.

Transfer to Slo-Cooker. In the same pan, sauté the onions and carrots gently for 3–4 minutes. Stir in the flour then slowly mix in the chicken stock, redcurrant jelly, seasoning and bay leaf. Bring to the boil and transfer to Slo-Cooker. Stir the mixture well.

To prepare the stuffing, mix together the breadcrumbs, onion, sage and seasoning, and bind with the beaten egg. Add a little milk if necessary.

Form the stuffing into eight balls and arrange on top of the pork mixture in the Slo-Cooker. Cook on High for 30 minutes then switch to Low for 5–8 hours. Remove bay leaf before serving.

COOKING TIME
Pre-heat 20 minutes
High 30 minutes
Low 5–8 hours

Hot Spare Ribs

 Serves 6

INGREDIENTS	Imperial	Metric	American
Pork spare ribs	2½ lb.	1 kg.	2½ lb.
Seasoned flour			
Cooking oil	2 tbsp.	30 ml.	2 tbsp.
Onion, finely chopped	1	1	1
Green pepper, de-seeded and finely chopped	1	1	1
Clove garlic, crushed	1	1	1
Beer	½ pt.	300 ml.	1¼ cups
Tomato purée or paste	2 tbsp.	2 tbsp.	2 tbsp.
Worcestershire sauce	4 tbsp.	4 tbsp.	4 tbsp.
Tabasco sauce	4–5 drops	4–5 drops	4–5 drops

Pre-heat Slo-Cooker on High for 20 minutes. Coat the spare ribs with seasoned flour. Heat the cooking oil in a large pan and brown the spare-ribs quickly on all sides. Transfer to Slo-Cooker. In the same pan, sauté the onion, pepper and garlic gently for 3–4 minutes. Stir in the remaining ingredients, bring to the boil and pour over the spare-ribs in the Slo-Cooker. Cook on High for 30 minutes, then switch to Low for 5–8 hours.

COOKING TIME
Pre-heat 20 minutes
High 30 minutes
Low 5–8 hours

POULTRY AND GAME

Slow cooked poultry and game is deliciously moist and tender, with none of the drying out that normally takes place during conventional cooking. Roasting birds or boiling fowl are cooked perfectly in the Slo-Cooker. The flesh of game and boiling fowl is often tough enough to require long cooking anyway, and the Slo-Cooker will tenderise gently and slowly, and all the flavour is sealed in the pot.

Whole birds and joints may be prepared in your Slo Cooker and many different recipes are given here. The size of your Slow Cooker will of course dictate the size of the bird you cook. A 4½ lb. (2 kg) chicken fits snugly into a 6 pint (3.5 litre) pot.

Try Parsley Roast Chicken as an introduction to slow cooking poultry and taste the difference.

YOUR FREEZER AND SLOW COOKED POULTRY AND GAME

Frozen poultry and game must be completely thawed before cooking.

Poultry and game dishes are most successful freezing candidates. Special instructions are given where necessary in the following recipes.

Frozen poultry dishes are best thawed at room temperature and reheated gently in the oven just before serving.

CHECKPOINTS FOR SLOW COOKING POULTRY AND GAME

To improve the flavour and appearance of the finished dish, poultry and game require light browning in a separate pan before slow cooking.

Cut vegetables into small pieces to ensure even cooking.

Whole poultry is best trussed for slow cooking to enable easy removal from the pot, particularly if a recipe is left to cook for longer than intended.

Avoid considerable overcooking of poultry. The flesh remains beautifully succulent and tasty of course but when the bones begin to fall apart after long cooking they can prove annoying.

When adapting your own recipes for slow cooking do not be heavy-handed with the seasoning. It is better to adjust seasoning to taste before serving.

Remember to use less liquid (about half normally) since little is lost through evaporation.

Liquids used may be stock, water, wine, cider or fruit juice.

Thickening agents such as flour or cornflour may be added to the dish at the start of cooking (as in most of the recipes to follow) or at the end (follow the instructions on page 10). Egg yolks, cream and milk should not be added till about 30 minutes before serving.

For guidance on cooking times when adapting your own recipes consult a similar recipe in this section.

The Slo-Cooker may be filled to within ½–1 inch (1–2½ cm.) of the brim.

Spicy Chicken

 Serves 4

INGREDIENTS	Imperial	Metric	American
Butter	2 oz.	50 g.	¼ cup
Chicken joints	4	4	4
Onion, chopped	1	1	1
Sticks or stalks celery, chopped	2	2	2
Flour	2 tbsp.	2 tbsp.	2 tbsp.
Chicken stock	¼ pt.	150 ml.	⅔ cup
Canned pineapple pieces	15½ oz.	439 g.	medium can
Chilli powder	1½ tsp.	1½ tsp.	1½ tsp.
Ground ginger	½ tsp.	½ tsp.	½ tsp.
Salt	1 tsp.	1 tsp.	1 tsp.
Black pepper	½ tsp.	½ tsp.	½ tsp.
Tabasco sauce	few drops	few drops	few drops

Pre-heat Slo-Cooker on High for 20 minutes. Heat the butter in a large pan and brown the chicken joints on all sides. Transfer to Slo-Cooker. In the same butter sauté the onion and celery until beginning to turn transparent. Stir in the flour then the chicken stock slowly. Add the pineapple (including juice) and remaining ingredients. Bring to the boil, stirring continuously.

Pour this sauce over the chicken in the Slo-Cooker. Cook on High for 30 minutes then switch to Low for 4–6 hours. Serve with plenty of green salad.

COOKING TIME
Pre-heat 20 minutes
High 30 minutes
Low 4–6 hours

Pheasant in Cider

 Serves 4

INGREDIENTS	Imperial	Metric	American
Large pheasant	1	1	1
Seasoned flour			
Butter	4 oz.	100 g.	¼ lb.
Onion, finely chopped	1	1	1
Garlic clove, crushed	1	1	1
Flour	2 tbsp.	2 tbsp.	2 tbsp.
Dry cider	½ pt.	300 ml.	1¼ cups
Bouquet garni			
Salt and pepper			
Streaky bacon rashers or slices	4	4	4
Eating apples	2	2	2
Soured cream	4 tbsp.	4 tbsp.	4 tbsp.
Paprika pepper	1 tsp.	1 tsp.	1 tsp.

Pre-heat Slo-Cooker on High for 20 minutes.
Dust the pheasant with seasoned flour. Heat half the butter in a large pan and brown the pheasant on all sides. Transfer to Slo-Cooker. In the same butter sauté the onion and garlic gently until transparent. Stir in the flour then gradually add the cider, bouquet garni and seasoning. Bring to the boil, stirring all the time. Pour round the pheasant. Cook on High for 30 minutes then switch to Low for 5–7 hours. Place the pheasant on a serving dish. Roll the bacon rashers and sauté in the remaining butter. Core the apples and cut each into eight pieces. Sauté in the butter until golden brown. Use these to garnish the pheasant. Strain the liquid from the pheasant and stir in soured cream and paprika. Serve separately.

COOKING TIME
Pre-heat 20 minutes
High 30 minutes

Low 5–7 hours, depending on size of bird

Coq-au-Vin

 Serves 4

INGREDIENTS	Imperial	Metric	American
Butter	*2 oz.*	*50 g.*	*¼ cup*
Chicken joints	*4*	*4*	*4*
Onion, chopped	*2*	*2*	*2*
Clove garlic, crushed	*1*	*1*	*1*
Rashers or slices	*6*	*6*	*6*
* streaky bacon,*			
* chopped*			
Flour	*2 oz.*	*50 g.*	*½ cup*
Chicken stock	*¼ pt.*	*150 ml.*	*⅔ cup*
Red wine	*½ pt.*	*300 ml.*	*1¼ cups*
Button mushrooms,	*4 oz.*	*100 g.*	*¼ lb.*
* halved*			
Salt and black pepper			
Bay leaves	*2*	*2*	*2*
Bouquet garni	*1*	*1*	*1*

Pre-heat Slo-Cooker on High for 20 minutes. Heat the butter in a large pan and brown the chicken joints on all sides. Transfer to Slo-Cooker. In the same butter sauté the onion, garlic and bacon gently until beginning to turn transparent. Stir in the flour then gradually add the chicken stock and red wine.

Bring to the boil, stir in the remaining ingredients then transfer to Slo-Cooker. Cook on High for 30 minutes then switch to Low for 6–8 hours. Before serving remove the bay leaves and bouquet garni.

COOKING TIME   High 30 minutes
Pre-heat 20 minutes   Low 6–8 hours

TO FREEZE
Omit garlic. Pack into rigid polythene or foil container, cover and freeze. Add garlic or garlic salt at reheating stage.

Chicken with Barbecue Sauce

 Serves 4

INGREDIENTS	Imperial	Metric	American
Butter	1½ oz.	40 g.	3 tbsp.
Chicken	2½–3 lb.	1–1½ kg.	2½–3 lb.
Salt and pepper			
Small onion, finely chopped	1	1	1
Tomato ketchup	4 tbsp.	4 tbsp.	4 tbsp.
Vinegar	2 tbsp.	2 tbsp.	2 tbsp.
Mango chutney, chopped	2 tbsp.	2 tbsp.	2 tbsp.
French mustard	½ tsp.	½ tsp.	½ tsp.
Caster or superfine sugar	1 tsp.	1 tsp.	1 tsp.
Worcestershire sauce	1 tbsp.	1 tbsp.	1 tbsp.

Rub the inside of the Slo-Cooker with a little of the butter then pre-heat on High for 20 minutes.

Wipe the chicken and season it inside and out with salt and pepper. Heat the remaining butter in a large pan and brown the chicken all over. Transfer to Slo-Cooker. In the same butter sauté the onion gently for 2–3 minutes. Add the remaining ingredients to the onion and bring to the boil. Pour the sauce over the chicken. Cook on High for 3 hours, basting 2–3 times if possible.

COOKING TIME
Pre-heat 20 minutes
High 3 hours

TO FREEZE
Leftover slices of chicken may be frozen in foil trays with the sauce poured over. Cover and freeze.

Chicken Casserole

  Serves 4

INGREDIENTS

	Imperial	Metric	American
Butter	2 oz.	50 g.	$\frac{1}{4}$ cup
Chicken joints	4	4	4
Onions, chopped	2	2	2
Clove garlic, crushed	1	1	1
Rashers or slices streaky bacon, chopped	2	2	2
Carrots, chopped	2 large	2 large	2 large
Sticks or stalks celery, chopped	2	2	2
Flour	2 tbsp.	2 tbsp.	2 tbsp.
Chicken stock	$\frac{3}{4}$ pt.	400 ml.	2 cups
Tomato purée or paste	2 tbsp.	2 tbsp.	2 tbsp.
Salt and pepper			
Bouquet garni			
Frozen sweetcorn and peppers	8 oz.	226 g.	$\frac{1}{2}$ lb.

Pre-heat Slo-Cooker on High for 20 minutes. Heat the butter in a large pan and brown the chicken joints well on all sides. Transfer to Slo-Cooker. In the same butter sauté the onions, garlic, bacon, carrots and celery gently for 3–4 minutes. Stir in the flour then slowly add the chicken stock, stirring well. Add the tomato purée seasoning and bouquet garni and bring to boil, stirring continuously.

Pour the sauce over the chicken in the Slo-Cooker. Cook on High for 30 minutes then switch to Low for 6–8 hours. Remove bouquet garni and adjust seasoning if necessary. $\frac{1}{2}$–1 hour before serving stir in the defrosted sweetcorn and peppers.

COOKING TIME
Pre-heat 20 minutes
High 30 minutes
Low 6–8 hours

TO FREEZE
Omit garlic. Pack into rigid polythene or foil container cover and freeze. Add garlic at reheating stage, or season with garlic salt.

Turkey Supreme

  Serves 6

INGREDIENTS	Imperial	Metric	American
Butter	1 oz.	25 g.	2 tbsp.
Turkey breasts, cut into pieces or	4	4	4
turkey drumsticks	6	6	6
Onion, thinly sliced	1	1	1
Sticks or stalks celery, chopped	4	4	4
Carrots, diced	2	2	2
Flour	2 tbsp.	2 tbsp.	2 tbsp.
Chicken stock	½ pt.	300 ml.	1¼ cups
Bouquet garni			
Salt and pepper			
Single or thin cream	¼ pt.	150 ml.	⅔ cup

Pre-heat Slo-Cooker on High for 20 minutes.
Heat the butter in a large pan and sauté the turkey gently for 2–3 minutes. Transfer to Slo-Cooker. In the same butter sauté the onion, celery and carrots for a further 2–3 minutes. Stir in the flour then gradually add the chicken stock, bouquet garni and seasoning. Bring to the boil stirring continuously and pour over the turkey. Cook on High for 30 minutes then switch to Low for 6–8 hours. 30 minutes before serving stir in the cream.
Garnish with grilled bacon rolls.

COOKING TIME
Pre-heat 20 minutes
High 30 minutes
Low 6–8 hours

TO FREEZE
Omit cream, pack in rigid polythene or foil containers, cover and freeze. Add cream on reheating.

Parsley Roast Chicken

  Serves 6

INGREDIENTS	Imperial	Metric	American
Roasting chicken	4 lb.	1.8 kg.	4 lb.
Clove garlic, cut into slithers	1 large	1 large	1 large
Salt			
Black pepper, freshly ground			
Cooking oil	4 tbsp.	60 ml.	4 tbsp.
Butter	4 oz.	100 g.	¼ lb.
Chopped parsley	3 tbsp.	3 tbsp.	3 tbsp.

Pre-heat Slo-Cooker on High for 20 minutes.
Using a sharp knife cut small slits in the breasts and thighs of the chicken and insert the slithers of garlic. Season the bird with salt and freshly ground black pepper. Heat the cooking oil and butter in a large pan and brown the chicken well on all sides. Lift into Slo-Cooker. Stir the parsley into the remaining oil and butter and use it to coat the chicken. Cook on High for 4–5 hours.

COOKING TIME
Pre-heat 20 minutes
High 4–5 hours

TO FREEZE
Leftover slices or portions may be frozen in foil trays.

Chicken Parcels

 Serves 4

INGREDIENTS	Imperial	Metric	American
Rashers or slices streaky bacon	4	4	4
Chicken thighs, skinned	8	8	8
Butter	1 oz.	25 g.	2 tbsp.
Onions, chopped	2	2	2
Clove garlic, crushed	1	1	1
Cornflour or cornstarch	1 tbsp.	1 tbsp.	1 tbsp.
Canned tomatoes	14 oz.	397 g.	medium can
Chicken stock	$\frac{1}{4}$ pt.	150 ml.	$\frac{2}{3}$ cup
Bay leaf	1	1	1
Dried oregano	2 tsp.	2 tsp.	2 tsp.
Salt and pepper			

Pre-heat Slo-Cooker on High for 20 minutes. Cut the bacon rashers in half and trim off the rind. Wrap one bacon piece around each chicken thigh and arrange in the Slo-Cooker. Heat the butter in a pan and gently sauté the onions and garlic until transparent. Mix in the corflour then slowly stir in the tomatoes (including juice) and chicken stock. Add remaining ingredients, bring to the boil and pour over the chicken in the Slo-Cooker. Cook on High for 30 minutes then switch to Low for 3–4 hours.

COOKING TIME
Pre-heat 20 minutes
High 30 minutes   Low 3–4 hours

TO FREEZE
Omit garlic. Arrange the chicken parcels in foil container, pour sauce over, cover and freeze. Defrost and reheat in same container, adding crushed garlic or garlic salt.

Duck in Orange

  Serves 4

INGREDIENTS

	Imperial	Metric	American
Cooking oil	1 tbsp.	1 tbsp.	1 tbsp.
Duck	4½ lb.	2 kg.	4½ lb.
Butter	1 oz.	25 g.	2 tbsp.
Onions, finely chopped	2	2	2
Mushrooms sliced thinly	4 oz.	100 g.	¼ lb.
Flour	1 oz.	25 g.	¼ cup
Frozen orange juice, diluted	¾ pt.	400 ml.	2 cups

Pre-heat Slo-Cooker on High for 20 minutes. Heat the cooking oil in a large pan and brown the duck well on all sides. Transfer to Slo-Cooker. Do not add any fat. Cook on High for 30 minutes then switch to Low for 6–8 hours. Drain off the fat and discard. Heat the butter in pan and sauté the onions and mushrooms until soft. Stir in the flour then gradually add the orange juice. Bring to the boil, stirring continuously and pour over the duck. Cook on Low for a further 2 hours.

COOKING TIME
Pre-heat 20 minutes
High 30 minutes
Low 6–8 hours plus 2 hours

TO FREEZE
Leftover slices of duck may be frozen in foil trays with orange sauce poured over.

VEGETABLES

Vegetable flavours are delicate, so it is good to know that they are sealed in during slow cooking and gently but surely developed within the pot. You will probably find the texture differs slightly to vegetables cooked conventionally but you will most certainly note and appreciate the improved flavours.

Fresh, frozen, and dried vegetables are suitable for slow cooking. Refer to the following list of checkpoints for guidance.

Of the recipes in this section, some can be eaten as an appetiser, some as a main course, and others as an accompaniment to a main course. I hope you will enjoy menu-mixing and trying your own vegetable recipes in the Slo-Cooker.

YOUR FREEZER AND SLOW COOKED VEGETABLES

Frozen vegetables should be thawed before adding to the Slo-Cooker. In order to retain their full colour and texture, stir them into a recipe during the final $\frac{1}{2}$–1 hour of cooking. This will also avoid suddenly and drastically lowering the temperature within the Slo-Cooker.

Slow cooked vegetables can be frozen, particularly if cooked in a sauce, though you may not feel it is worth it for some recipes. Remember that vegetables tend to lose some of their flavour and texture on freezing and reheating. Suitable recipes for freezing have been marked in this section.

CHECKPOINTS FOR SLOW COOKING VEGETABLES

Generally speaking vegetables require long cooking times in the Slo-Cooker. It is important therefore to cut them into fairly small pieces. A thickness of $\frac{1}{4}$ inch ($\frac{1}{2}$ cm.) is a good standard. This applies particularly when the recipe combines root vegetables and meat.

Root vegetables such as potatoes, carrots, turnips, swede, onion etc. usually require a cooking period of at least 6 hours on Low setting.

Ensure even cooking by cutting the vegetables evenly.

Quickly-cooked vegetables can be added to a recipe $\frac{1}{2}$–1 hour before serving.

Remember to include less seasoning—the vegetables will retain all their own concentrated flavour. Adjustments can always be made at the end of the cooking period.

Remember also, when adapting your own recipes for slow cooking, to reduce the amount of liquid used. It is worth noting however that some vegetables are liable to dry up on the outside and discolour if not covered with liquid. Additionally they will not cook in the recommended time. These include potatoes and other root vegetables. You will probably find you need fewer vegetables to flavour a recipe, particularly the stronger types, such as onions and leeks.

Generally, dried vegetables should be pre-soaked with bicarbonate of soda before slow cooking. To ensure thorough cooking of dried vegetables they should be boiled in water for 10–15 minutes before adding to the Slo-Cooker. Then make sure they are immersed in the cooking liquid.

Thickening agents (flour and cornflour) can be added at the start of cooking. Add cream, milk and egg yolks during the final 30 minutes.

Cabbage Cup

 Serves 4

INGREDIENTS

	Imperial	Metric	American
Medium white cabbage	$\frac{1}{2}$	$\frac{1}{2}$	$\frac{1}{2}$
Smoked bacon, cut into small pieces	12 oz.	350 g.	$\frac{3}{4}$ lb.
Butter	1 oz.	25 g.	2 tbsp.
Black pepper			
Ground cummin	$\frac{1}{2}$ tsp.	$\frac{1}{2}$ tsp.	$\frac{1}{2}$ tsp.
Ground turmeric	$\frac{1}{4}$ tsp.	$\frac{1}{4}$ tsp.	$\frac{1}{4}$ tsp.
Bacon or chicken stock			

Pre-heat Slo-Cooker on High for 20 minutes. Scoop the centre from the cabbage, leaving a 'cup' at least $\frac{1}{2}$ in./1 cm. thick, and immerse in boiling water for 2–3 minutes. Finely shred about one-third of the cabbage core. Place the bacon pieces in a pan and pour over sufficient cold water to cover. Bring slowly to the boil, discard the water and dry the bacon pieces on kitchen paper.

Heat the butter in a large pan and sauté the bacon for 2–3 minutes. Season with black pepper and stir in the cummin, turmeric and shredded cabbage. Place this mixture into the cabbage and stand it in the Slo-Cooker. Pour round sufficient stock to come half way up the sides of the cabbage. Cook on High for 30 minutes then switch to Low for 6–9 hours. Serve on a bed of freshly boiled vegetables.

COOKING TIME
Pre-heat 20 minutes
High 30 minutes
Low 6–9 hours

Pease in the Pot

 Serves 4–6

INGREDIENTS

	Imperial	Metric	American
Dried peas	8 oz.	225 g.	$\frac{1}{2}$ lb.
Bicarbonate of soda	1 tsp.	1 tsp.	1 tsp.
Butter	1 oz.	25 g.	2 tbsp.
Streaky bacon rashers or slices chopped	4	4	4
Water	$\frac{3}{4}$ pt.	400 ml.	2 cups
Salt			
Black pepper			

Soak peas overnight with the bicarbonate of soda in 1 pt./500 ml./$2\frac{1}{2}$ cups water.

Pre-heat Slo-Cooker on High for 20 minutes.

Drain the peas then boil in plenty of water for 10 minutes.

Heat the butter in a pan and sauté the chopped bacon gently for 2–3 minutes. Add the drained peas, water and seasoning. Bring to the boil then transfer to Slo-Cooker. Cook on Low for 8–12 hours.

COOKING TIME
Pre-heat 20 minutes
Low 8–12 hours

TO FREEZE
Pack into rigid polythene or foil container, cover and freeze.

Courgettes Hereford

 Serves 4–6

INGREDIENTS	Imperial	Metric	American
Butter	1½ oz.	40 g.	3 tbsp.
Courgettes, cut into	1 lb.	450 g.	1 lb.
1 in./2½ cm lengths			
Garlic clove, crushed	1	1	1
Small onion, chopped finely	1	1	1
Cornflour or cornstarch	1 tbsp.	1 tbsp.	1 tbsp.
Apple juice	½ pt.	300 ml.	1¼ cups
Salt			
Black pepper			
Tomatoes, skinned and sliced	2–3	2–3	2–3

Pre-heat Slo-Cooker on High for 20 minutes.
Heat the butter in a large pan and sauté the courgettes quickly till lightly browned. Transfer to Slo-Cooker. In the same fat sauté the garlic and onion gently until they begin to turn transparent. Add the cornflour then carefully stir in the apple juice. Season with salt and pepper, stir in the tomatoes, and bring to the boil (stirring continuously). Pour the sauce over the courgettes and cook on Low for 4–6 hours. The courgettes should have a slight bite.

COOKING TIME
Pre-heat 20 minutes
Low 4–6 hours

Ratatouille

 Serves 6

INGREDIENTS	Imperial	Metric	American
Cooking oil	3 tbsp.	3 tbsp.	3 tbsp.
Onions, chopped	2	2	2
Garlic clove, crushed	1	1	1
Tomatoes, skinned and sliced	1 lb.	450 g.	1 lb.
Aubergines, sliced	2	2	2
Courgettes, sliced	4	4	4
Green peppers, deseeded and sliced	2	2	2
Tomato purée or paste	3 tbsp.	3 tbsp.	3 tbsp.
Salt			
Black pepper, freshly ground			

Pre-heat Slo-Cooker on High for 20 minutes.
Heat the cooking oil in a large pan and sauté the onion and garlic until transparent. Stir in the remaining ingredients, seasoning to taste with salt and black pepper. Cook for a further 2–3 minutes then transfer to Slo-Cooker. Cook on Low for 6–9 hours.

COOKING TIME
Pre-heat 20 minutes
Low 6–9 hours.

TO FREEZE
Pack in rigid polythene or foil container, cover and freeze.

German Bean Casserole

 Serves 4–6

INGREDIENTS	Imperial	Metric	American
Butter beans	*8 oz.*	*225 g.*	*½ lb.*
Bicarbonate of soda	*1 tsp.*	*1 tsp.*	*1 tsp.*
Butter	*1 oz.*	*25 g.*	*2 tbsp.*
Cooking oil	*1 tbsp.*	*1 tbsp.*	*1 tbsp.*
Onions, large thinly sliced	*2*	*2*	*2*
Clove garlic, crushed	*1*	*1*	*1*
Can tomatoes	*14 oz.*	*396 g.*	*medium*
Chicken stock	*¼ pt.*	*150 ml.*	*⅔ cup*
Salt			
Freshly ground black pepper			
Smoked German sausage, sliced	*8 oz.*	*225 g.*	*½ lb.*

Soak the beans in 1 pt./500 ml./2½ cups water with the bicarbonate of soda overnight.

Pre-heat Slo-Cooker on High for 20 minutes. Drain the beans then boil in plenty of water for 10 minutes. Heat the butter and cooking oil in a large pan. Sauté the onions and garlic until transparent. Add the remaining ingredients, including the drained beans and bring to the boil. Transfer to Slo-Cooker. Cook on High for 30 minutes then switch to Low for 7–8 hours. Stir before serving.

COOKING TIME
Pre-heat 20 minutes
High 30 minutes
Low 7–8 hours

TO FREEZE
Omit garlic and sausage. Pack into rigid polythene or foil container, cover and freeze. Add garlic and sausage during reheating.

Italian Stuffed Peppers

 Serves 4

INGREDIENTS

	Imperial	Metric	American
Macaroni, thin-cut, quick-cook	2 oz.	50 g.	2 oz.
Cooking oil	2 tbsp.	2 tbsp.	2 tbsp.
Onion, medium diced	1	1	1
Clove garlic, crushed	1	1	1
Minced beef	1 lb.	450 g.	1 lb.
Flour	2 tbsp.	2 tbsp.	2 tbsp.
Tomato purée or paste	2 tsp.	2 tsp.	2 tsp.
Tomato ketchup	2 tbsp.	2 tbsp.	2 tbsp.
Beef stock	$\frac{1}{4}$ pt.	150 ml.	$\frac{2}{3}$ cup
Button mushrooms, diced	4 oz.	100 g.	$\frac{1}{4}$ lb.
Mixed herbs	$\frac{1}{2}$ tsp.	$\frac{1}{2}$ tsp.	$\frac{1}{2}$ tsp.
Large green peppers	4	4	4

Pre-heat Slo-Cooker on High for 20 minutes.
Boil the macaroni in slightly salted water until just tender. Drain. Heat the cooking oil in a large pan and sauté the onion and garlic until transparent. Add the beef and continue cooking for 2–3 minutes. Stir in the flour, tomato purée, tomato ketchup and beef stock. Boil until thickened then add the mushrooms, herbs and drained macaroni. Remove the stalk and cut the cap from the top of each pepper; remove the seeds. Fill the peppers with the beef mixture and stand them in the Slo-Cooker. Pour round $\frac{1}{4}$ pt./150 ml./$\frac{2}{3}$ cup slightly salted water. Cook on High for 30 minutes then switch to Low for 4–5 hours.

COOKING TIME
Pre-heat 20 minutes
High 30 minutes
Low 4–5 hours

CHECKPOINT
Do not allow the peppers to touch the walls of the Slo-Cooker as they will burn.

Cabbage Turnovers

 Serves 6

INGREDIENTS

	Imperial	Metric	American
Cooking oil	2 tbsp.	2 tbsp.	2 tbsp.
Chopped onion	2 tbsp.	2 tbsp.	2 tbsp.
Garlic clove (optional) crushed	1	1	1
Minced beef, lean	1 lb.	450 g.	1 lb.
Tomatoes, skinned and chopped	2	2	2
Cooked rice	1 oz.	25 g.	2–3 tbsp.
Salt and pepper			
Mixed herbs	1 tsp.	1 tsp.	1 tsp.
Chopped parsley	2 tbsp.	2 tbsp.	2 tbsp.
Cabbage leaves, medium-sized	12	12	12
Can tomatoes, or	14 oz.	396 g.	medium can
can condensed tomato soup	10$\frac{1}{2}$ oz.	298 g.	medium can

Pre-heat Slo-Cooker on High for 20 minutes.
 Heat the cooking oil in a large pan and sauté the onion and garlic (optional) gently until transparent. Add the minced beef and cook till browned. Stir in the tomatoes, rice, seasoning, herbs and parsley and mix together well. Dip the cabbage leaves in boiling water for about 2 minutes, drain and dry with kitchen paper. Place some of the mince mixture in the centre of each leaf and roll up, tucking under the ends to form a parcel. Place these in the Slo-Cooker. Heat the tomatoes (roughly chopped and juice included) or tomato soup in a saucepan and pour over the cabbage. Cook on Low for 3$\frac{1}{2}$–5 hours.

COOKING TIME
Pre-heat 20 minutes

Low 3$\frac{1}{2}$–5 hours

Tuna-stuffed Marrow

 Serves 6

INGREDIENTS

	Imperial	Metric	American
Can tuna fish	7 oz.	198 g.	medium
Onion, finely chopped	1	1	1
Long-grain rice, cooked	4 tbsp.	4 tbsp.	4 tbsp.
Salt and pepper			
Chopped parsley	1 tbsp.	1 tbsp.	1 tbsp.
Juice of lemon	$\frac{1}{2}$	$\frac{1}{2}$	$\frac{1}{2}$
Marrow, medium-large	1	1	1

Pre-heat Slo-Cooker on High for 20 minutes.
 Drain and flake the tuna fish and mix with the onion, rice, seasoning, parsley and lemon juice. Cut of the ends of the marrow and trim the length so that it will stand upright in the Slo-Cooker. Scoop out the seeds using a spoon. Fill the marrow with the fish mixture and wrap it in buttered foil. Stand the marrow in the Slo-Cooker and pour round $\frac{1}{2}$ pt./300 ml./1$\frac{1}{4}$ cups boiling water. Cook on Low for 8–10 hours. Serve with tomato sauce if liked.

COOKING TIME
Pre-heat 20 minutes
Low 8–10 hours

Winter Potato Casserole

 Serves 4–6

INGREDIENTS	Imperial	Metric	American
Butter	2 oz.	50 g.	$\frac{1}{4}$ cup
Onion, small grated	1	1	1
Carrot, large grated	1	1	1
Old Potatoes, grated	1 lb.	450 g.	1 lb.
Ground mace	$\frac{3}{4}$ tsp.	$\frac{3}{4}$ tsp.	$\frac{3}{4}$ tsp.
Salt			
Black pepper, freshly ground			
Canned condensed Cream of Chicken Soup	10$\frac{1}{2}$ oz.	298 g.	medium can
Water	$\frac{1}{4}$ pt.	150 ml.	$\frac{2}{3}$ cup

Pre-heat Slo-Cooker on High for 20 minutes.

Heat the butter in a large pan and gently sauté the onion, carrot and potatoes for 4–5 minutes. Add the mace and season with salt and black pepper. Mix together the chicken soup and water and add to the pan. Bring slowly to the boil, stirring well all the time and transfer to Slo-Cooker. Cook on Low for 6–8 hours.

COOKING TIME
Pre-heat 20 minutes
Low 6–8 hours

Leek and Cider Hotpot

 Serves 6

INGREDIENTS	Imperial	Metric	American
Butter	2 oz.	50 g.	$\frac{1}{4}$ cup
Bacon, chopped	4 oz.	100 g.	$\frac{1}{4}$ lb.
Leeks, chopped	2 lb.	1 kg.	2 lb.
Eating apples, peeled, cored and sliced	2	2	2
Cider	1 pt.	500 ml.	2$\frac{1}{2}$ cups
Flour	3 tbsp.	3 tbsp.	3 tbsp.

Pre-heat Slo-Cooker on High for 20 minutes.

Heat the butter in a large pan and sauté the chopped bacon gently for 2–3 minutes. Stir in the leeks and apples. Mix a little cider with the flour to form a smooth paste. Add the rest of the cider to the flour mixture then pour this onto the leeks. Bring to the boil, stirring continuously. Transfer to Slo-Cooker. Cook on Low for 6–10 hours.

Serve with hot crusty bread rolls.

COOKING TIME
Pre-heat 20 minutes
Low 6–10 hours

TO FREEZE
Pack into rigid polythene or foil container, cover and freeze.

Greek Mushrooms

Serves 8

INGREDIENTS	Imperial	Metric	American
Cooking oil	*2 tbsp.*	*2 tbsp.*	*2 tbsp.*
Onion, finely chopped	*1*	*1*	*1*
Clove garlic, crushed	*1*	*1*	*1*
Button mushrooms	*1½ lb.*	*700 g.*	*1½ lb.*
Canned tomatoes	*10 oz.*	*397 g.*	*medium can*
Salt	*2 tsp.*	*2 tsp.*	*2 tsp.*
Black pepper, freshly ground			
Chopped parsley			

Pre-heat Slo-Cooker on High for 20 minutes.
Heat the cooking oil in a large pan and sauté the onion and garlic gently until beginning to turn transparent. Add the mushrooms, tomatoes and salt, and season to taste with black pepper. Bring to the boil and transfer to Slo-Cooker. Cook on Low for 2–3 hours. Stir in the parsley before serving.

Superb as a vegetable accompaniment or as an appetiser with hot toast or crusty bread. Can be served hot or cold.

COOKING TIME
Pre-heat 20 minutes
Low 2–3 hours

TO FREEZE
Pack into rigid polythene container, cover and freeze. Thaw in room temperature.

DESERTS

Traditional puddings and desserts are no longer just memories of childhood when you have a Slo-Cooker. Your own pudding recipes, for example, can easily be adapted for slow cooking. Just follow the recipes in this section for guidance. Timing is not nearly so crucial as with conventional cooking.

Slo-Cooked fruit is 'something special'. Its flavour is gently developed within the pot while the fruit remains beautifully whole for serving. Fruit flavours, spices etc. complement each other to produce a subtle end to a meal.

The Slo-Cooker is ideal for preparing pie, pudding and crumble fillings. Just place the fruit, water and spices in the Slo-Cooker and leave to cook while you are otherwise occupied.

Fruit and delicate desserts such as egg custard, ideally require careful, long cooking without the risk of overcooking. They are therefore perfectly suited to slow cooking since the timing is more flexible than during conventional cooking.

Cookers with removable pots facilitate the addition of a topping to be crisped up in a hot oven or under a hot grill. In Slo-Cookers with permanently fixed pots, a base (such as fruit) could be prepared in the Slo-Cooker while the cook is away from home, then finished off later in a separate dish with a meringue or crumble topping.

Try cooking your Christmas Pud' in the Slo-Cooker. You will find the flavour is remarkably traditional. Just imagine all the fruit flavours, spices and brandy developing and blending for all those hours. The result can be nothing other than superb. An added bonus is that you need not worry about the Slo-Cooker boiling dry; and there is none of the steam which normally fills the kitchen during Christmas Pud' preparation.

YOUR FREEZER AND SLOW COOKED DESSERTS

Suet puddings are best frozen uncooked and should be thawed before slow cooking. Sponge puddings may be frozen raw or cooked. Leftover sponge pudding may be frozen and then reheated in the Slo-Cooker. Just place the pudding in an ovenproof dish, cover with foil, and pour boiling water round. Heat on Low for 1–2 hours depending on the amount being reheated.

Fruits cooked in the Slo-Cooker remain whole, so are ideally suited to freezing. Frozen fruit for pies, crumbles etc. is a great standby.

Cooked egg custards and milk puddings are not suitable for freezing. However, uncooked egg custard can be frozen; thaw before slow cooking.

CHECKPOINTS FOR SLOW COOKED DESSERTS

When adapting your own recipes for the Slo-Cooker remember:
fresh fruit will require less cooking liquid (water, wine etc.) since there is less evaporation;
dried fruit should be covered with liquid if it is to cook evenly;
pour boiling water round steamed puddings to set them off to a good start;
steamed puddings should be cooked on the High setting;
when slow cooking steamed puddings, do not fill the basin more than two thirds full—allow the pudding space to rise; it is a good idea to make a pleat in the foil or greaseproof paper covering.

Gooseberry Pie

 Serves 4

INGREDIENTS	Imperial	Metric	American
Gooseberries	12 oz.	350 g.	$\frac{3}{4}$ lb.
Sugar	2 oz.	50 g.	$\frac{1}{4}$ cup
Chopped walnuts	1 oz.	25 g.	$\frac{1}{4}$ cup
Topping :			
Self-raising flour or flour sifted with 1 tsp. baking powder	4 oz.	100 g.	1 cup
Suet, shredded or chopped	2 oz.	50 g.	$\frac{1}{3}$ cup
Caster or superfine sugar	1 oz.	25 g.	2 tbsp.
Milk	4 tbsp.	4 tbsp.	4 tbsp.
Whipped cream to decorate			
Chopped walnuts to decorate			

Pre-heat Slo-Cooker on High for 20 minutes.
Lightly butter an ovenproof dish to just fit the Slo-Cooker. Arrange the gooseberries in the dish and sprinkle with the sugar and walnuts.

To make the topping, sieve the flour and stir in the suet and sugar. Beat in the milk to make a firm dough. Roll out the dough into a circle on a lightly floured board to fit the dish. Lay the topping on the gooseberries and cover the basin with buttered the gooseberries and cover the basin with buttered foil. Stand the pudding in the Slo-Cooker and pour round sufficient water to come half way up the sides of the basin. Cook on High for 3–4 hours. Decorate with whipped cream and chopped walnuts to serve.

COOKING TIME
Pre-heat 20 minutes
High 3–4 hours

Almond Rhubarb Pudding

 Serves 4

INGREDIENTS	Imperial	Metric	American
Rhubarb, cut into 1 inch/$2\frac{1}{2}$ cm. sticks	1 lb.	450 g.	1 lb.
Sugar	3 tbsp.	3 tbsp.	3 tbsp.
Margarine	4 oz.	100 g.	$\frac{1}{2}$ cup
Soft brown sugar	4 oz.	100 g.	$\frac{1}{2}$ cup
Eggs, beaten	2	2	2
Almond essence	2 tsp.	10 ml.	2 tsp.
Self-raising flour or flour sifted with $1\frac{1}{2}$ tsp. baking powder	6 oz.	175 g.	$1\frac{1}{2}$ cups
Cocoa powder	3 tsp.	3 tsp.	3 tsp.
Ground nutmeg	1 tsp.	1 tsp.	1 tsp.

Lightly butter the inside of Slo-Cooker and pre-heat on High for 20 minutes. Arrange the rhubarb in the base of the Slo-Cooker and sprinkle with the sugar. In a basin, cream the margarine and sugar until light and fluffy. Gradually beat in the eggs and almond essence. Sieve together the flour, cocoa powder and nutmeg and fold in gently. Spread the mixture over the rhubarb. Cover gently with a piece of buttered greaseproof paper (butter side down). Cook on High for 3–4 hours.

COOKING TIME
Pre-heat 20 minutes
High 3–4 hours

Ginger Rhubarb

 Serves 4

INGREDIENTS	Imperial	Metric	American
Rhubarb, cut into 1 in./ 2½ cm. lengths	1 lb.	450 g.	1 lb.
Water	¼ pt.	150 ml.	⅔ cup
Sugar	4 tbsp.	4 tbsp.	4 tbsp.
Rind and juice of orange	1	1	1
Preserved stem ginger, thinly sliced, and its syrup	2 oz. 3 tsp.	50 g. 3 tsp.	¼ cup 3 tsp.

Place all ingredients in the Slo-Cooker and mix well. Cook on Low for 4–6 hours. Delicious served well chilled with whipped cream.

COOKING TIME
Low 4–6 hours

Note: If your Slo-Cooker has a removable pot try pouring off a little of the juice, adding a meringue or crumble topping and finishing off in the oven. Alternatively, pour off some of the juice, transfer the fruit to another ovenproof dish, add the topping and finish off in the oven.

Fruit Salad

 Serves 4

INGREDIENTS

	Imperial	Metric	American
Mixed dried fruit, such as apricots, prunes, peaches, apple rings, raisins	*8 oz.*	*225 g.*	*½ lb.*
Demerara or brown sugar	*1–2 tbsp.*	*1–2 tbsp.*	*1–2 tbsp.*
Water, cider or wine, or mixture	*1 pt.*	*600 ml.*	*2½ cups*
Grated rind of lemon	*½*	*½*	*½*
Grated rind of orange	*1*	*1*	*1*

Arrange the dried fruit in the Slo-Cooker and sprinkle over the sugar. Mix remaining ingredients together and pour over the fruit. Cook on Low for 8–10 hours. Serve hot with custard sauce or chilled with whipped cream.

COOKING TIME
Low 8–10 hours

TO FREEZE
Pack in rigid polythene container, cover and freeze.

Apricot Bread and Butter Pudding

  Serves 4-6

INGREDIENTS	Imperial	Metric	American
Thin slices buttered bread	6-8	6-8	6-8
Canned apricots	14½ oz.	411 g.	medium can
Caster or superfine sugar	2 tbsp.	2 tbsp.	2 tbsp.
Eggs, beaten	3	3	3
Few drops almond essence			
Milk	¾ pt.	400 ml.	2 cups

Pre-heat Slo-Cooker on High for 20 minutes.
Line a suitable ovenproof dish with the slices of bread (buttered side down). Drain the apricots and, reserving 5 or 6 for decoration, chop finely and scatter over the bread. Arrange any remaining bread on the fruit. Beat together the sugar, eggs and almond essence. Warm the milk to blood heat and pour onto the eggs. Pour this mixture over the bread and apricots. Cover the dish securely with buttered foil. Stand the dish in the Slo-Cooker and pour round sufficient boiling water to come half way up the sides. Cook on Low for 4-6 hours. Before serving decorate the top of the pudding with remaining apricots.

COOKING TIME
Pre-heat 20 minutes
Low 4-6 hours

Baked Custard

  Serves 4

INGREDIENTS	Imperial	Metric	American
Eggs	4	4	4
Sugar, caster or superfine	2 oz.	50 g.	¼ cup
Milk	1 pt.	550 ml.	2½ cups
Few drops vanilla essence			
Grated nutmeg			

Pre-heat Slo-Cooker on High for 20 minutes.
Blend together the eggs and sugar. Warm the milk to blood heat and pour onto the eggs. Add the vanilla essence. Pour the custard into a 1½ pt./1 litre/4 cup ovenproof dish. Sprinkle with grated nutmeg and cover with buttered foil. Stand the dish in the Slo-Cooker and pour round sufficient boiling water to come half way up its sides. Cook on Low for 3-4 hours. A knife inserted in the centre of the custard should come out clean.

COOKING TIME
Pre-heat 20 minutes
High 3-4 hours

Orange Rice Pudding

 Serves 6

INGREDIENTS	Imperial	Metric	American
Butter	1 oz.	25 g.	2 tbsp.
Milk	1½ pt.	900 ml.	3¾ cups
Evaporated milk	¼ pt.	150 ml.	⅔ cup
Pudding rice	4 heaped tbsp.	4 heaped tbsp.	4 heaped tbsp.
Sugar	4 tbsp.	4 tbsp.	4 tbsp.
Grated rind and juice of orange	1	1	1
Few drops vanilla essence			

Grease the inside of the Slo-Cooker with the butter. Put all the ingredients into the Slo-Cooker and mix well. Cook on Low for 5–8 hours.

COOKING TIME
Low 5–8 hours

Chocolate Sauce

 Serves 4–6

INGREDIENTS	Imperial	Metric	American
Plain or dark cooking chocolate	4 oz.	100 g.	¼ lb.
Juice of orange	1	1	1
Butter, cut into small pieces	1 oz.	25 g.	2 tbsp.
Golden syrup	4 tbsp.	4 tbsp.	4 tbsp.

Break the chocolate into squares and place all the ingredients in the Slo-Cooker. Cook on Low for 2–6 hours. Stir well before serving.

COOKING TIME
Low 2–6 hours

Note: try stirring some sliced bananas into the sauce 30 minutes before serving; or serve with ice cream.

Honey Topped Pudding

 Serves 4

INGREDIENTS	Imperial	Metric	American
Soft honey	2–3 tbsp.	2–3 tbsp.	2–3 tbsp.
Chopped walnuts	2 tbsp.	2 tbsp.	2 tbsp.
Butter	4 oz.	100 g.	½ cup
Sugar, caster or superfine	4 oz.	100 g.	½ cup
Eggs, beaten	2	2	2
Self-raising flour or flour sifted with 1½ tsp. baking powder	6 oz.	175 g.	1½ cups
Milk to mix			

Pre-heat Slo-Cooker on High for 20 minutes.
Mix together the honey and walnuts and pour into a buttered 1½ pt./1 litre/4 cup basin. Beat together the butter and sugar till light and creamy. Gradually beat in the eggs. Sieve the flour and gently fold into the mixture. Add a little milk if necessary to form a smooth dropping consistency. Put the mixture into the prepared basin and cover with lightly buttered foil. Stand the basin in the Slo-Cooker and pour round sufficient boiling water to come half way up the sides. Cook on High for 2–3 hours. Turn out and serve with custard sauce or fresh cream.

COOKING TIME
Pre-heat 20 minutes
High 2–3 hours

Pears Beaujolais

 Serves 4

INGREDIENTS	Imperial	Metric	American
Red wine	¾ pt.	400 ml.	2 cups
Sugar	6 oz.	175 g.	¾ cup
Grated rind and juice of lemon	1	1	1
Cloves	2	2	2
A little red food colouring			
Pears, peeled, whole	4	4	4

Put the first five ingredients into the Slo-Cooker and mix together well. Place the pears in the Slo-Cooker, stalks upwards, and baste with the wine mixture. Cook on Low for 5–6 hours, turning the pears occasionally to make sure they are coated in the syrup and colour evenly. Remove the cloves before serving. Delicious hot or chilled with cream.

COOKING TIME
Low 5–6 hours

Crème Caramel

  Serves 4–6

INGREDIENTS

	Imperial	Metric	American
Sugar	8 tbsp.	8 tbsp.	8 tbsp.
Water	$\frac{1}{4}$ pt.	150 ml	$\frac{2}{3}$ cup
Milk	1 pt.	500 ml.	$1\frac{1}{4}$ cups
Eggs	4	4	4
Few drops vanilla essence			

Pre-heat Slo-Cooker on High for 20 minutes. To make the caramel, heat together 2 tbsp. of the sugar with the water in a small pan. Boil rapidly and when it begins to turn golden brown (caramelises) pour the caramel into a warmed soufflé dish. Allow it to cool.

Beat together the milk, eggs, vanilla essence and remaining sugar. Bring to blood heat then strain onto the caramel. Cover with foil and stand the container in the Slo-Cooker. Pour round sufficient boiling water to come half way up the sides of the container and cook on Low for 3–4 hours.

COOKING TIME
Pre-heat 20 minutes
Low 3–4 hours

CHECKPOINT
Crème Caramel must be chilled for several hours before being turned out of its container. It helps to gently ease the custard away from the dish.

Cooking times may vary with the type and size of dish used. Your will no doubt experiment to find the correct time for your particular dish.

Lemon Sponge

   Serves 4

INGREDIENTS

	Imperial	Metric	American
Butter	4 oz.	100 g.	$\frac{1}{2}$ cup
Sugar, caster or superfine	4 oz.	100 g.	$\frac{1}{2}$ cup
Eggs, beaten	3	3	3
Rind and juice of lemons	2	2	2
Milk	$\frac{1}{2}$ pt.	300 ml.	$1\frac{1}{4}$ cups
Self-raising flour or flour sifted with 1 tsp. baking powder	4 oz.	100 g.	1 cup

Pre-heat Slo-Cooker on High for 20 minutes.
Cream the butter and sugar until light and fluffy. Gradually beat in the eggs. Stir in the lemon rind and juice and milk then quickly but gently fold in the sieved flour. Put the mixture into a buttered $1\frac{1}{2}$ pt./1 litre/4 cup basin and cover with buttered foil. Stand the basin in the Slo-Cooker and pour round sufficient water to come half way up the sides. Cook on High for 3–3$\frac{1}{2}$ hours. Serve with whipped cream or ice cream.

COOKING TIME
Pre-heat 20 minutes
High 2$\frac{1}{2}$–3$\frac{1}{2}$ hours

Christmas Pudding

 Serves 6

INGREDIENTS

	Imperial	Metric	American
Plain flour	2 oz.	50 g.	$\frac{1}{2}$ cup
Mixed spice	$\frac{1}{2}$ tsp.	$\frac{1}{2}$ tsp.	$\frac{1}{2}$ tsp.
Cinnamon	$\frac{1}{2}$ tsp.	$\frac{1}{2}$ tsp.	$\frac{1}{2}$ tsp.
Grated nutmeg	$\frac{1}{2}$ tsp.	$\frac{1}{2}$ tsp.	$\frac{1}{2}$ tsp.
Fresh white breadcrumbs	2 oz.	50 g.	1 cup
Shredded or finely chopped suet	5 oz.	150 g.	1 cup
Soft brown sugar	4 oz.	100 g.	$\frac{1}{2}$ cup
Raisins	6 oz.	175 g.	1 cup
Sultanas	6 oz.	175 g.	1 cup
Mixed peel	1 oz.	25 g.	$\frac{1}{4}$ cup
Ground almonds	1 oz.	25 g.	$\frac{1}{4}$ cup
Large eggs	2	2	2
Finely grated peel and juice of orange	$\frac{1}{2}$	$\frac{1}{2}$	$\frac{1}{2}$
Black treacle	$\frac{1}{2}$ tbsp.	$\frac{1}{2}$ tbsp.	$\frac{1}{2}$ tbsp.
Brandy or dry sherry	1 tbsp.	1 tbsp.	1 tbsp.
Almond essence	$\frac{1}{2}$ tsp.	$\frac{1}{2}$ tsp.	$\frac{1}{2}$ tsp.
Beer	2 fl. oz.	50 ml.	$\frac{1}{3}$ cup

Pre-heat Slo-Cooker on High for 20 minutes.
Sieve together the flour, spice, cinnamon and nutmeg then mix in the other dry ingredients. Beat together the eggs, orange peel and juice, treacle, brandy or sherry, almond essence and beer. Add this to the dry ingredients and mix well. Place the mixture into a buttered 2 pt./1 litre/2$\frac{1}{2}$ cup basin and cover securely with buttered foil. Stand the basin in the Slo-Cooker and pour round sufficient boiling water to come two thirds of the way up the sides. Cook on High for 3 hours then switch to Low for 14–18 hours, or cook on High for 11–12 hours.

COOKING TIME
Pre-heat 20 minutes
High 3 hours
Low 14–18 hours } or High 11–12 hours

CHECKPOINT
Ideally Christmas Pud' should be prepared in October. To store: cool and turn out the pudding and wrap in greaseproof paper with an outer layer of foil. To re-heat the pudding pre-heat the Slo-Cooker on High for 20 minutes. Place the pudding in its basin, cover with foil, and stand inside the Slo-Cooker. Pour round sufficient boiling water to come halfway up the sides and heat for about 6 hours on Low, or 4 hours on High.

COMPLETE MEALS

Here are some recipes specifically developed to provide a complete meal in itself. No accompaniments are needed. You can of course use many of the soup, vegetable, meat or poultry recipes in the previous sections—either as they stand or with simple, favourite additions. If your Slo-Cooker has a removable pot, try a casserole with a topping such as pastry, scone or buttered bread. They can then be crisped in the oven or under a pre-heated grill. Add dumplings to a soup or stew to make a warm and substantial meal. Simply put the dumplings in the Slo-Cooker for the final 30 minutes and cook on High setting.

Use the Slo-Cooker, too, in conjunction with other cooking equipment. Let the main course look after itself in the Slo-Cooker while you prepare an unusual or time-consuming appetiser or dessert. This is particularly handy if one course requires special last minute attention by the cook. You will find that less time is spent in the kitchen and more with your family and friends.

In the same way, a Slo-Cooker can be a boon when cooking facilities are in short supply—in a bedsitter perhaps, where there may only be one or two cooking rings. Entertaining is made considerably simpler if one course can be left to cook in the Slo-Cooker.

Experience will soon guide you as to what can be cooked and what cannot.

An ordinary occasion can be made into a party (or a plain meal into a feast) by using the Slo-Cooker for something a little special. For example, try a hot relish or dip to accompany sausages, beefburgers or fish fingers.

Finally, slow cooking is not just a British tradition. Many foreign dishes are designed for this particular method of cooking; so try preparing your favourites in your Slo-Cooker.

Continental Macaroni Cheese

  Serves 4–6

INGREDIENTS	Imperial	Metric	American
Macaroni	8 oz.	225 g.	½ lb.
Canned sweet pimentos, chopped	6¾ oz.	190 g.	small can
Bierwurst, thinly sliced	8 oz.	225 g.	½ lb.
Butter	2 oz.	50 g.	¼ cup
Flour	2 oz.	50 g.	½ cup
Milk	1¼ pt.	700 ml.	3 cups
Salt			
Black pepper			
Made mustard	1 tsp.	1 tsp.	1 tsp.
Cheese, grated	4 oz.	100 g.	¼ lb.

Butter the inside of the Slo-Cooker lightly and pre-heat on High for 20 minutes.

Boil the macaroni in lightly salted water for 4–5 minutes, drain and dry. Mix together the macaroni, pimentos and Bierwurst and place in the Slo-Cooker. Heat the butter in a saucepan and stir in the flour. Carefully stir in the milk and season with salt, black pepper and mustard. Bring to the boil, stirring continuously. Pour the sauce over the macaroni and cook on Low for 3–4 hours.

COOKING TIME
Pre-heat 20 minutes
Low 3–4 hours

TO FREEZE
Left-over macaroni cheese may be frozen in foil dishes. To reheat, place the covered, thawed dish in the Slo-Cooker and pour boiling water round. Heat on Low for 1–2 hours depending on quantity.

Chilli Con Carné

 Serves 4

INGREDIENTS	Imperial	Metric	American
Dried red kidney beans	8 oz.	225 g.	½ lb.
Bicarbonate of soda or baking soda	1 tsp.	1 tsp.	1 tsp.
Butter	1 oz.	25 g.	2 tbsp.
Onions, chopped	2	2	2
Minced beef	1 lb.	450 g.	1 lb.
Canned tomatoes	14 oz.	397 g.	medium can
Tomato purée or tomato paste	1 tbsp.	1 tbsp.	1 tbsp.
Salt and pepper			
Chilli powder	2½ tsp.	2½ tsp.	2½ tsp.
Malt vinegar	1 tbsp.	1 tbsp.	1 tbsp.
Sugar	2 tsp.	2 tsp.	2 tsp.

Place the beans in a bowl and well cover them with water. Add the bicarbonate of soda. Leave to soak overnight.

Pre-heat Slo-Cooker on High for 20 minutes. Strain the beans, then boil in plenty of water for 15 minutes. Heat the butter in a large pan and sauté the onions gently until transparent. Stir in the minced beef and brown lightly. Add the remaining ingredients and bring to the boil. Transfer to Slo-Cooker. Cook on High for 30 minutes then switch to Low for 8–10 hours. Stir well before serving.

COOKING TIME High 30 minutes
Pre-heat 20 minutes Low 8–10 hours

TO FREEZE
Pack into rigid polythene or foil container, pack and freeze.

Lasagne

 Serves 6

INGREDIENTS

	Imperial	Metric	American
Lasagne	8 oz.	225 g.	½ lb.
Butter	1 oz.	25 g.	2 tbsp.
Large onion, chopped finely	1	1	1
Large clove garlic, crushed	1	1	1
Mince	1¼ lb.	550 g.	1¼ lb.
Oregano	2 tsp.	2 tsp.	2 tsp.
Salt			
Freshly ground black pepper			
Tomatoe purée or paste	4 tbsp.	4 tbsp.	4 tbsp.
Cheese sauce :			
Butter	1 oz.	25 g.	2 tbsp.
Flour	1 oz.	25 g.	¼ cup
Milk	½ pt.	300 ml.	1¼ cups
Salt and pepper			
Grated cheese	4 oz.	100 g.	¼ lb.
Parmesan cheese for topping			

Grease the inside of the Slo-Cooker and Pre-heat on High for 20 minutes. Boil the lasagne sheets in lightly salted water for 4–5 minutes to soften, then dry with kitchen paper. Heat the butter in a large pan and gently sauté the onion and garlic until transparent. Add the mince and oregano and cook for a further 3–4 minutes, stirring well. Season with salt and pepper and add the tomato purée.

To make the cheese sauce, heat the butter in a saucepan and stir in the flour. Gradually add the milk, stirring well, then bring slowly to the boil, still stirring. Season with salt and pepper and add the cheese.

Arrange a layer of mince mixture in the Slo-Cooker, followed by a layer of pasta, then cheese sauce. Continue doing this, finishing with a layer of cheese sauce. Sprinkle parmesan cheese over the top and cook on Low for 4–6 hours.

COOKING TIME
Pre-heat 20 minutes
Low 4–6 hours

NOTE: If your Slo-Cooker is fitted with a removable pot the Lasagne may be browned in a hot oven or under the grill.

TO FREEZE
Leftover lasagne may be frozen in foil dishes. Thaw before reheating in the Slo-Cooker. To reheat: place the foil dish (covered) in the Slo-Cooker and pour round boiling water. Heat on Low (times will depend on the amount being reheated).

Chicken Risotto

 Serves 4

INGREDIENTS

	Imperial	Metric	American
Cooking oil	2 tbsp.	2 tbsp.	2 tbsp.
Onions, finely chopped	2	2	2
Chicken stock	1½ pt.	900 ml.	2¾ cups
Green pepper, deseeded and finely chopped	1	1	1
Button mushrooms, chopped	4 oz.	100 g.	¼ lb.
Tomatoes, skinned and chopped	3	3	3
Easy-cook long grain rice	6 oz.	175 g.	¾ cup
Cooked chicken, chopped	8 oz.	225 g.	½ lb.
Cooked ham, chopped	2 oz.	50 g.	2 oz.

Pre-heat Slo-Cooker on High for 20 minutes. Heat the cooking oil in a large pan and sauté the onions gently until beginning to soften. Add the stock and bring to the boil. Stir in remaining ingredients, bring to the boil again and transfer to Slo-Cooker. Cook on Low for 3–4 hours. Stir before serving.

COOKING TIME
Pre-heat 20 minutes
Low 3–4 hours

Winter Casserole

  Serves 6

INGREDIENTS

	Imperial	Metric	American
Cooking oil	3 tbsp.	3 tbsp.	3 tbsp.
Stewing beef, cut into cubes	2 lb.	1 kg.	2 lb.
Onions, chopped	2	2	2
Celery sticks or stalks, chopped	2	2	2
Carrots, thinly sliced	4	4	4
Large potatoes, cut into ½ in./1 cm. cubes	3	3	3
Flour	1 oz.	25 g.	2 tbsp.
Beef stock	¾ pt.	400 ml.	2 cups
Salt and pepper			
Bouquet garni			

Pre-heat Slo-Cooker on High for 20 minutes.
Heat the cooking oil in a large pan and brown the meat lightly. Transfer to Slo-Cooker. In the same oil sauté the vegetables for about 5 minutes. Mix the flour with a little of the beef stock to form a smooth paste. Add the rest of the stock then pour over the vegetables, Add seasoning and bouquet garni. Bring to the boil then transfer to Slo-Cooker. Stir the mixture well. Cook on High for 30 minutes then switch to Low for 6–10 hours.

COOKING TIME
Pre-heat 20 minutes
High 30 minutes
Low 6–10 hours

TO FREEZE
Pack in rigid polythene or foil container, cover and freeze.

Paella

 Serves 6

INGREDIENTS

	Imperial	Metric	American
Cooking oil	2 tbsp.	2 tbsp.	2 tbsp.
Onion, finely chopped	1	1	1
Garlic clove, crushed	1	1	1
Chicken stock	1½ pt.	900 ml.	2¾ cups
Pinch powdered saffron			
Easy-cook long grain rice	8 oz.	225 g.	1¼ cups
Tomatoes, skinned and chopped	4	4	4
Red pepper, deseeded and finely chopped	1	1	1
Cooked chicken, chopped	8 oz.	225 g.	½ lb.
Cooked mussels	6–8	6–8	6–8
Salt			
Black pepper			
Frozen peas, thawed	8 oz.	225 g.	½ lb.
Prawns	4 oz.	100 g.	¼ lb.

Pre-heat Slo-Cooker on High for 20 minutes.
  Heat the cooking oil in a large pan and sauté the onion and garlic until beginning to soften. Add the chicken stock and saffron and bring to the boil. Add remaining ingredients, except peas and prawns, and bring to the boil again. Transfer to Slo-Cooker. Cook on Low for 3–4 hours. 30 minutes before serving, stir in the peas and prawns.

COOKING TIME
Pre-heat 20 minutes
Low 3–4 hours

PRESERVES

The preparation of fruit and vegetables for preserves can be a time-consuming affair, and it normally requires constant attention from the cook. Now fruit and vegetables can be softened in the Slo-Cooker while you are out of the house or in bed. For example, mixtures softened overnight are ready for final boiling or reduction in the morning.

In jam-making the slow, gentle cooking in the Slo-Cooker along with the least small amount of liquid means that the full flavour and pectin content are extracted from the fruit. The fruit remains attractively whole and the little amount of liquid used means less boiling is needed after the sugar has been added. The final boiling is the only part of the jam-making that requires attention.

CHECKPOINTS FOR SLOW COOKED JAM AND MARMALADE

Choose fresh, ripe, firm, unblemished fruit for a perfect result.

Softening the fruit helps to release the setting agent (pectin) naturally present in fruit. Some fruits contain more than others, and you may need to mix fruits or to add lemon juice to make up for the lack of pectin in one. High-pectin fruits include blackcurrants, redcurrants, damsons and goosberries. Medium-pectin fruits include apricots, greengages, loganberries, plums and raspberries. Low-pectin fruits include blackberries, cherries, marrow, pears, rhubarb and strawberries.

Warmed sugar will take less time to dissolve and will produce a preserve of better flavour and colour.

After final boiling of the softened fruit and sugar in an open saucepan there are three methods of checking that the jam or marmalade has reached setting point:

1. The temperature test is the most reliable method. The jam will set when it reaches a temperature of 221 F (104 C).

2. Place a little jam on to a cold plate. When it has cooled push your finger across the surface of the jam. If it wrinkles then you have a set. During this test it is a good idea to move the pan off the heat to avoid boiling the jam too long.

3. Stir the jam or marmalade with a wooden spoon and lift it out. The jam will begin to set on the spoon when setting point is reached.

Note: when making strawberry or raspberry jam, reduce the liquid by half.

Orange Marmalade

 Makes about 6 lb./2.6 kg.

INGREDIENTS	Imperial	Metric	American
Seville oranges	*2 lb.*	*1 kg.*	*2 lb.*
Lemon	*1*	*1*	*1*
Boiling water	*3 pt.*	*1.5 litre*	*7½ cups*
Sugar	*4 lb.*	*2 kg.*	*8 cups*

Pre-heat Slo-Cooker on High for 20 minutes. Carefully remove the peel from the oranges and lemon. Use a sharp knife or potato peeler to make sure no pith is attached. Chop the peel finely. Squeeze the juice from them. Place the fruit juice, peel and 2½ pt./1.5 litres/6¾ cups of the boiling water into the Slo-Cooker. Cook on Low for 7–10 hours.

Place the remaining water, pips and coarsely chopped pith into a large saucepan and simmer for about 45 minutes. Strain the mixture and add the contents of the Slo-Cooker and the sugar to the liquid. Heat gently, stirring well, until the sugar dissolves then boil rapidly until setting point is reached (see page 104). Allow to stand until a skin forms then pour into heated jars and cover with wax discs. Cover when cool.

COOKING TIME
Low 7–10 hours

Jam

 Makes about 3 lb./1.5 kg.

INGREDIENTS	Imperial	Metric	American
Fruit, prepared according to kind	*2 lb.*	*1 kg.*	*2 lb.*
Water	*½ pt.*	*300 ml.*	*1¼ cups*
Sugar	*2 lb.*	*1 kg.*	*4 cups*

Place the fruit and water in the Slo-Cooker. Cook on Low for 8–10 hours. Transfer the cooked mixture to a large pan and stir in the warmed sugar. Heat gently, stirring well to dissolve the sugar. Boil rapidly until setting point is reached (see page 104). Pour the jam into warmed jars and cover with wax discs, and cover.

COOKING TIME
Low 8–10 hours

Lemon Curd

   Makes 2 lb./1 kg.

INGREDIENTS

	Imperial	Metric	American
Butter	4 oz.	100 g.	$\frac{1}{2}$ cup
Grated rind and juice of lemons	4	4	4
Sugar, caster or superfine	1 lb.	450 g.	2 cups
Eggs, lightly beaten	4	4	4

Pre-heat Slo-Cooker on High for 20 minutes. Heat the butter in a saucepan and add the lemon rind and juice and sugar. Heat gently, stirring, until the sugar dissolves. Allow to cool. Stir the eggs into the cooled mixture and pour into a 2 pt./1 litre/5 cup basin. Cover with foil. Stand the basin in the Slo-Cooker and pour round sufficient boiling water to come half way up the sides. Cook on Low for 3–4$\frac{1}{2}$ hours. The mixture should be thick. Allow to cool

COOKING TIME
Low 3–4$\frac{1}{2}$ hours

Apple Chutney

Makes 4–5 lb./1.8–2.3 kg.

INGREDIENTS

	Imperial	Metric	American
Apples, peeled, cored and chopped	3 lb.	1.4 kg.	3 lb.
Onions, finely chopped	1 lb.	450 g.	1 lb.
Soft brown sugar	1$\frac{1}{2}$ lb.	1.4 kg.	3 cups
Sultanas	8 oz.	225 g.	$\frac{1}{2}$ lb.
Vinegar	$\frac{1}{2}$ pt.	300 ml.	1$\frac{1}{4}$ cups
Large clove garlic, crushed	1	1	1
Salt	1 tbsp.	1 tbsp.	1 tbsp.
Cayenne pepper, pinch			
Pickling spice	2 tsp.	2 tsp.	2 tsp.

Place all ingredients (except spice) in the Slo-Cooker and mix well. Tie the spice in a piece of muslin and add to the chutney. Cook on Low for 10–12 hours. If convenient, stir twice during this time. Remove the spice bag and pour the chutney into heated jars and cover.

COOKING TIME
Low 10–12 hours

Dried Apricot Jam

 Makes about 6 lb./2.6 kg.

INGREDIENTS	Imperial	Metric	American
Dried Apricots	1 lb.	450 g.	1 lb.
Water	2 pt.	1 litre	5 cups
Juice of lemon	1	1	1
Sugar	3 lb.	1.3 kg.	3 lb.
Blanched almonds	2–3 oz.	50–75 g.	2–3 oz.

Place the fruit, water and lemon juice in the Slo-Cooker and cook on Low for 8–10 hours. Transfer the cooked mixture to a large pan and stir in the warmed sugar. Heat gently, stirring well to dissolve the sugar. Boil rapidly until setting point is reached (see page 104). Pour the jam into warmed jars, cover with waxed discs and covers.

COOKING TIME
Low 8–10 hours

LITTLE EXTRAS

The recipes in this section emphasise the versatility of the Slo-Cooker. They are perhaps recipes one would not bother to prepare under normal circumstances, but because they can be prepared in the Slo-Cooker without careful attendance, are made simple and convenient.

Surprise your family with 'real' porridge for breakfast, cooked overnight in the Slo-Cooker. On more exotic lines, try heating drinks and punches to greet you late on Halloween, or after a November 5th bonfire. Christmas too is a good time to use your Slo-Cooker as a centrepiece with Spiced Wine. Celebrate a birthday with Cider Punch.

Slo-Cook Gingerbread is delicious. The texture and flavour are perfect; and though the surface of the cake does not crisp and brown, the addition of a glaze gives a most attractive finish.

You will no doubt discover other uses for your Slo-Cooker. If it is kept handy on a work surface you will be tempted to use it as often as possible. Hopefully this chapter will help stimulate ideas to do just that.

Slo-Cook Gingerbread

 Serves 8–10

INGREDIENTS

	Imperial	Metric	American
Dark soft brown sugar	8 oz.	225 g.	1 cup
Butter	6 oz.	175 g.	$\frac{3}{4}$ cup
Golden syrup	12 oz.	350 g.	$\frac{3}{4}$ lb.
Flour	1 lb.	450 g.	1 lb.
Salt	1 tsp.	1 tsp.	1 tsp.
Ground ginger	3–4 tsp.	3–4 tsp.	3–4 tsp.
Baking powder	2 tsp.	2 tsp.	2 tsp.
Egg	1	1	1
Milk	$\frac{1}{2}$ pt.	300 ml.	$1\frac{1}{4}$ cups
Chopped peel and cherries, mixed	1 tbsp.	1 tbsp.	1 tbsp.
To glaze :			
Sugar	2 oz.	50 g.	4 tbsp.
Water	2 tbsp.	2 tbsp.	2 tbsp.

Pre-heat Slo-Cooker on High for 20 minutes. Lightly butter a 7 in./15 cm. round cake tin (preferably non-stick). In a saucepan, melt the sugar, butter and syrup gently until the sugar is dissolved. Allow to cool. Sieve the dry ingredients into a basin, make a well in the centre and pour in the melted mixture, egg and milk. Stir well to form a smooth consistency. Pour the mixture into the prepared tin and sprinkle the chopped peel and cherries over the top. Cover with buttered foil and stand the tin in the Slo-Cooker. Pour round sufficient water to come half way up the sides of the tin. Cook on High for 5–8 hours. Turn the gingerbread out of the tin. Blend together the sugar and water and brush it over the top of the gingerbread immediately. Allow to cool

COOKING TIME
Pre-heat 20 minutes
High 5–8 hours

TO FREEZE
Interleave slices of gingerbread with greaseproof paper and wrap securely in foil. This way, individual servings may be taken from the freezer.

CHECKPOINT
Invert a small, ovenproof container in the Slo-Cooker, to lift the tin clear of the base and to assist its easy removal.

Porridge

 Serves 4

INGREDIENTS

	Imperial	Metric	American
Water	$1\frac{1}{2}$ pt.	900 ml.	$3\frac{3}{4}$ cups
Oatmeal	4 oz.	100 g.	$\frac{1}{4}$ lb.
Salt	$\frac{1}{2}$ tsp.	$\frac{1}{2}$ tsp.	$\frac{1}{2}$ tsp.

Pre-heat Slo-Cooker on High for 20 minutes. Boil the water in a saucepan and sprinkle the oatmeal over, stirring continuously. Add the salt then transfer to Slo-Cooker. Cook on Low for about 8 hours or overnight.

COOKING TIME
Pre-heat 20 minutes
Low 8 hours.

Marmalade Sauce

 Serves 8

INGREDIENTS

	Imperial	Metric	American
Water	$\frac{3}{4}$ pt.	400 ml.	2 cups
Marmalade	6 tbsp.	6 tbsp.	6 tbsp.
Rind of lemon, cut in strips	1	1	1
Sugar, caster or superfine	2 tbsp.	2 tbsp.	2 tbsp.
Arrowroot	2 tbsp.	2 tbsp.	2 tbsp.

Place the water, marmalade, lemon rind and sugar into the Slo-Cooker. Mix the arrowroot with about 2 tbsp. of cold water to make a smooth paste and stir into the marmalade mixture. Cook on High for 4–5 hours. Stir after 3 hours if possible. Serve with sponge or baked or steamed puddings.

COOKING TIME
High 4–5 hours

Note: this sauce can also be made using apricot jam or red jam instead of marmalade.

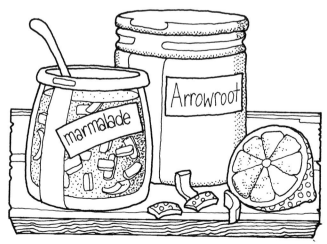

Tea Punch

INGREDIENTS

	Imperial	Metric	American
Tea	2 pt.	1 litre	5 cups
Red wine	1 pt.	500 ml.	2½ cups
Grated lemon rind and juice	1	1	1
Clear honey	4 tbsp.	4 tbsp.	4 tbsp.
Cinnamon stick			
Orange, sliced	1	1	1

Place all ingredients in the Slo-Cooker and heat on Low for 2 hours.

COOKING TIME
Low 2 hours

Cider Punch

INGREDIENTS

	Imperial	Metric	American
Eating apples	2	2	2
Cloves	8	8	8
Cider	3½ pt.	2 litre	9 cups
Cinnamon stick			
Ground ginger	2 tsp.	2 tsp.	2 tsp.
Brown sugar	4 tbsp.	4 tbsp.	4 tbsp.
Grated rind and juice of lemon	1	1	1

Cut the apples in half and remove the cores. Stick two cloves into the skin side of each half apple. Place all ingredients in the Slo-Cooker and heat on Low for 2 hours.

COOKING TIME
Low 2 hours

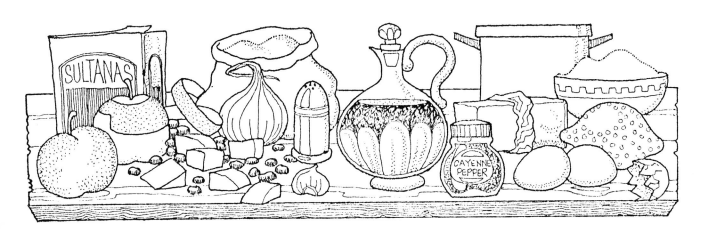

Home-made Tomato Juice

INGREDIENTS

	Imperial	Metric	American
Tomatoes, skinned and chopped	2 lb.	1 kg.	2 lb.
Onion, finely chopped	2 tbsp.	2 tbsp.	2 tbsp.
Salt	2 tsp.	2 tsp.	2 tsp.
Black pepper	½ tsp.	½ tsp.	½ tsp.
Sugar	1½ tbsp.	1½ tbsp.	1½ tbsp.
Lemon juice	1 tbsp.	1 tbsp.	1 tbsp.

Place all the ingredients into the Slo-Cooker and stir well. Cook on Low for 6–8 hours. Sieve the tomato juice, chill well and serve with Worcestershire Sauce.

COOKING TIME
Low 6–8 hours

Note: If the colour of the finished juice should need improving, use a little red food colouring or tomato purée or ketchup.

Cheese Fondue

  Serves 8–10

INGREDIENTS

	Imperial	Metric	American
Clove garlic, halved	1	1	1
Gruyere cheese, grated	1 lb.	450 g.	1 lb.
Emmenthal cheese, grated	1 lb.	450 g.	1 lb.
Cornflour or cornstarch	1 tbsp.	1 tbsp.	1 tbsp.
White pepper			
Grated nutmeg			
Dry white wine	½ pt.	300 ml.	1¼ cups

Rub the inside of the Slo-Cooker with the garlic. Mix together the cheeses, cornflour, pepper and nutmeg. Transfer to Slo-Cooker. Pour over the wine and cook on Low for 2–3 hours, stirring occasionally. Serve with pieces of crusty bread.

COOKING TIME
Low 2–3 hours

Orange and Lemonade Punch

INGREDIENTS	Imperial	Metric	American
Carton Frozen Orange juice	6¼ oz.	128 ml.	medium can
Lemonade	2 pt.	1 litre	5 cups
Orange, cut into 6–8 rings	1	1	1
Cloves	6–8	6–8	6–8
Cinnamon stick	3 in.	8 cm.	3 in.

Pour the thawed orange juice and lemonade into the Slo-Cooker and mix together well. Stick a clove in the centre of each orange ring and float these, along with the cinnamon stick, on top of the punch. Cook on Low for 2–3 hours.

COOKING TIME
Low 2–3 hours

Slo-Baked Apple

 Serves 4

INGREDIENTS	Imperial	Metric	American
Medium cooking apples, cored	4	4	4
Soft dark brown sugar	4 oz.	100 g.	½ cup
Mixed spice	1 tsp.	1 tsp.	1 tsp.
Sultanas	3–4 oz.	75–100 g.	½–⅔ cup
Boiling water	¼ pt.	150 ml.	⅔ cup

Butter the base of the Slo-Cooker and pre-heat on High for 20 minutes. Slit the skins once right round the centre of each apple. Mix together the sugar, spice and sultanas and fill the apples with this mixture. Arrange the apples in the Slo-Cooker (any remaining sugar/spice mixture may be scattered round them) and pour round the boiling water. Cook on Low for 4–6 hours. Serve with custard sauce or cream.

COOKING TIME
Pre-heat 20 minutes
Low 4–6 hours

Spiced Vinegar

INGREDIENTS

	Imperial	Metric	American
Vinegar	2 pt.	1 litre	5 cups
Peppercorns, white	6	6	6
Mixture of blade mace, whole allspice, cloves and cinnamon stick	1 oz.	25 g.	1 oz.

Place all the ingredients in the Slo-Cooker and stir. Cook on Low for 2–4 hours. Cool and strain the vinegar and use as required.

COOKING TIME
Low 2–4 hours

Note: If individual spices are not available, use 2 oz./50 g. of ready-prepared pickling spice.

Spiced Wine

INGREDIENTS

	Imperial	Metric	American
Red wine	3 pt.	1.7 litre	7½ cups
Water	¾ pt.	400 ml.	2 cups
Brandy (optional)	4 tbsp.	4 tbsp.	4 tbsp.
Rind and juice of lemon	1	1	1
Orange, sliced	1	1	1
Brown sugar	3 tbsp.	3 tbsp.	3 tbsp.
Mixed spice	1½ tsp.	1½ tsp.	1½ tsp.

Place all ingredients in the Slo-Cooker and heat on low for 2 hours.

COOKING TIME
Low 2 hours

WEIGHTS AND MEASURES

Ingredients used in the recipes to follow are given in Imperial, Metric and American measures. Generally speaking the Metric and American measures are not exact equivalents of their Imperial counterparts. I find it better to work in quantities which have been rounded off to convenient measures. Where I have felt it important to be accurate, exact equivalents are given. It is wise to follow one set of measures; do not skip from one set to another.

All spoon and cup measures are level unless otherwise stated.

The Imperial pint measures 20 fluid ounces; the American pint measures 16 fluid ounces.

When cans of food are included in a recipe, the weights given on the label are quoted—these are usually exact equivalents.

When converting your own recipes from Imperial to Metric, or vice versa, use the tables below as guidelines.

CAPACITY

Imperial	Metric
$\frac{1}{4}$ pt. (5 fl. oz.)	150 ml.
$\frac{1}{2}$ pt. (10 fl. oz.)	300 ml.
$\frac{3}{4}$ pt. (15 fl. oz.)	400 ml.
1 pt. (20 fl. oz.)	500–600 ml.
$1\frac{1}{2}$ pt.	900 ml.
$1\frac{3}{4}$ pt.	1 litre
2 pt.	1.1 litre

SPOON CAPACITY

1 level teaspoonful = 5 millilitres or 1 × 5 ml. spoonful.
2 level teaspoonsful = 10 ml. or 2 × 5 ml. sp.
1 level tablespoonful = 15 ml. or 1 × 15 ml. sp.

WEIGHT

Imperial	Metric
1 oz.	25 g.
2 oz.	50 g.
3 oz.	75 g.
4 oz.	100–125 g.
5 oz.	150 g.
6 oz.	175 g.
8 oz.	225 g.
10 oz.	275 g.
12 oz.	350 g.
14 oz.	400 g.
16 oz. (1 lb.)	450 g.
$1\frac{1}{2}$ lb.	700 g.
2 lb.	900 g. (1000 g. = 1 kg.)
3 lb.	1.4 kilograms (kg.)

INDEX

Printed by A. Wheaton & Co. Ltd., Exeter